PRAISE FOR JESSICA BELLINGER AND
THE HUMILITY PARADOX

"So excited for Jess' book! She is an amazing woman and is so successful in everything she works on. I have seen her run multiple successful businesses and what impresses me most is how she is always so readily available to help others on their projects. She has helped me multiple times in starting up my business and I have been so grateful for the time she takes to answer my questions because time is so so valuable."

—Cydne Morgan
Wedding Videographer and Owner of Cydne Robinson Films
www.cydnerobinsonfilms.com

"Jessica's determination to grow and desire to help are not only inspiring; they have been game-changers in her path and the ones that she has crossed. Jessica helped me on occasions where it felt like the mess/tech gods had cursed me. She offered her time and knowledge to 'figure it out,' and that meant the world to me."

—Paola Ohlson
Wedding Photographer and Owner of Ohlson Photography
www.ohlsonphotography.com

"Over the last four years, I've had the pleasure of watching Jessica grow from a timid young wife, a new mom and an aspiring entrepreneur to a woman that commands an audience and is fully confident in her various roles. Despite her personal growth in all of these areas and having launched her own successful vegan nail polish company, she has remained humble and has not abandoned her Christian principles. She's a real life role model and I am happy to call her a true friend!"

—Arlene Jacobs
Wedding Photographer and Owner of Arlene Jacobs Photography
www.arlenejacobs.co

"Jessica was so willing and encouraging when I sat and talked with her on an hour long call about ventures and life. I've always loved her creativity and was drawn to the energy she produced. Her life story is so interesting and different then most. I'm so excited to see her journey as she grows as a business owner, creative . . . and now, author!"

—Jade Gibson
Professional Violinist and Owner of Jade Strings
www.jadestrings.com

"*Self-realization by definition is 'fulfillment by oneself of the possibilities of one's character or personality'; this is vital in the realm of healing. Understanding our strengths and weaknesses aids in the process of healing our wounds, and it presents the possibility of moving forward. Humility means throwing away our egos and accepting that we are all flawed. Jessica has worked through her own flaws with vulnerability coupled with the intention of helping others grow; that's not an easy task. Her energy is empowering. I have watched her overcome her fears as a friend and mother. Her work consistently reminds me that being vulnerable isn't scary and success is possible with a little self-reflection and effort. I cannot wait to see what else she has to share!*"

—Saffron Jade + Lemonade
Medical Freedom and Human Rights Activist
www.saffronjadeandlemonade.com

"*Driven. Focused. 'Will make it happen' attitude. And so far her track record is incredible. This girl doesn't give up. I've had the privilege of seeing her in action a few times with her photography business. Always professional, always focused, and delivered INCREDIBLE images for clients. Jessica Bellinger as a friend is someone you're so proud of, and as an entrepreneur you wanna know 'how do you do it?!' I'm so thankful she's taken the time to put pen to paper and allow as many as possible to see what she's seen and what she's gathered from it. To be able to take those words of wisdom and apply it to their own dreams and aspirations! This is definitely something anyone with a goal can benefit from!*"

—Faith Roberts
Wedding Photographer and Owner of Roberts and Warwick Photography

"*Jessica explains how self-acceptance and self-love shouldn't equal compromising yourself and your goals. Younger generations need to understand this concept to achieve greatness. Furthermore, she illustrates the balance between achieving greatness while practicing humility.*"

—Grace Yerkes
Occupational Therapist

THE HUMILITY
PARADOX

Humble is the new successful.

HOW HUMBLE PEOPLE CAN BE
HAPPIER, ACHIEVE MORE, AND MAKE A
BETTER LIVING

THE HUMILITY
PARADOX

JESSICA BELLINGER

Jessica Bellinger Photography LLC
Melbourne, FL

JESSICA BELLINGER
photography

Jessica Bellinger Photography LLC
P.O. Box 120214
W. Melbourne. FL, 32912
www.JessicaBellinger.com

Send feedback to hello@jessicabellinger.com

Publisher's Cataloging-In-Publication Data

Names: Bellinger, Jessica, author.

Title: The humility paradox: how humble people can be happier, achieve more,
    and make a better living / Jessica Bellinger.

Description: [Melbourne, Florida]: Jessica Bellinger Photography LLC, [2020]

Identifiers: ISBN 9781735725109 (softcover) | ISBN 9781735725116 (casebound
    hardcover) | ISBN 9781735725123 (ebook)

Subjects: LCSH: Bellinger, Jessica--Psychology. | Humility--Psychological
aspects.

    | Pride and vanity--Psychological aspects. | Popular culture--Psychological
    aspects. | Happiness--Psychological aspects. | Success--Psychological aspects.

Classification: LCC BJ1533.H93 B45 2020 (print) | LCC BJ1533.H93

    (ebook) | DDC 179.9--dc23

DEDICATION

*To my husband Jeffry and our kids
Judah, Noah, and Oakley.*

GO BEYOND THE BOOK.

Be humble, learn confidence, get paid. Because anything is possible for the soul with humility. I'll show you how to embrace those new opportunities with my personal productivity course *Get It Done*. Check out www.TheHumilityParadox.com for more info.

CONTENTS

INTRODUCTION

I've always been confused about what purpose an introduction serves. Why can't we just call it a chapter, since it basically is one, right? Most books have one, so I wrote one too. I used to skip reading the introduction until I realized that an intro is the "pre-book" where the author sets the tone. So yes, you *need* to read my introduction, because it's full of important information. We will call this "chapter zero."

So why another book about humility? The topic might make you yawn, but I promise, your mind will get boggled. You will spot the ways pride has blocked you from what you want most. And if you keep your heart open, you'll receive the key to unlock inner peace and lasting joy in every area of life, from your finances to your friendships.

If you picked up this book and thought, *Being humbler will make me better than most people, I'm already pretty humble,* or *Just teach me how to* look *more humble . . .* well, I'm sorry, but you *for sure* need this book. We're going on a journey to understanding how humility truly works and where pride hides. Doing so is crucial to everlasting happiness. The journey never ends. Still, first things first.

WHAT IS HUMILITY?

All the definitions of humility I found online are so vague; you can interpret them however you want. Take this one from Wikipedia:

Humility—a low self-regard and sense of unworthiness.

Yikes. I don't want to be unimportant. Neither do you. So don't worry—this book explains humility in a non-off-putting way. I won't tell you to sell all your belongings and live off the land to become humble. You can live your normal life—rich, poor, middle class, whatever—and still practice humility. Because money and possessions have nothing to do with being humble. You can drive a Bentley and still be humble.

Humility is understanding we are made to love one another greatly. If you love greatly, you always put others before yourself. I don't mean work yourself to the bone so you have nothing left and can't carry on because you never helped yourself. Humility means you realize everyone deserves your time, that you are not too good for anyone else. Humility means you're not ashamed to be seen with someone deemed uncool or below your league. Humility might look like bringing that homeless woman to church without shame for what Susy and Joe will think with their two-story, four-bedroom, three-bathroom suburban townhouse. It might mean inviting a kind person you met at Walmart to dinner. Yes, the one wearing assless chaps, a cowboy hat, high heels, and sunglasses indoors. You are not above PeopleOfWalmart.com. Humility basks in the presence of the outcast. Humility treats every person like they're the most important person in the room. Even if by any objective standard they're definitely not.

The person who thinks they are too good, too busy, or too significant to give someone else the time of day has reached their lowest level. I am too good for no one. Not my enemies, not the druggie on the street begging for food. The fact that I might think I'm too good for them or that I have a superior character means I'm not and I don't. No one is above another. Every life has equal value, even if you're convinced someone else doesn't deserve that value because they cheated you, lied to you, or stole from you. Even humanity's worst need our mercy and, yes, our humility.

Another way to define humility is by what it is not. Humility is not self-pity. Focusing on our own problems is selfishness. Point blank. The "woe is me" mindset is not okay. What is okay is dealing with that problem, getting help, recognizing you have a hole in your heart, and filling it. Then moving on.

Just as humility doesn't mean wallowing in misery, humility also doesn't make a big deal of itself. *Wow, I am so humbled to go to Africa this year and help a tribe drill a well for clean drinking water.* No. Sorry. Good deeds alone don't win humble points, especially deeds done to humility-signal on social media. Please do good for the world. Just know that humility is when your heart is in all the right places when you do so.

I could get on a mountaintop and yell about why we all need humility until I'm blue in the face. I lived in pride most of my life before discovering how much it hurt me. Pride and bitterness ruin a person until they die, if they so let them. I self-destructed because I refused to take responsibility for the monster called ego.

This book shares what my experiences with pride and humility ultimately taught me about personal fulfillment and business success. But be aware: this is neither a memoir nor a "professional" book. I haven't exactly lived a remarkable life, and I'm not making seven figures or dripping in gold. I'm pretty ordinary in the hardships I've faced in my pretty safe country—the USA, baby! I haven't lived in war zones or ever feared for my life. So one might say I have it easy.

But I have learned the secrets of humility the hard way on more than one occasion. Life has kicked me in the face once or twice, generally because of my own decisions. As I said, I like to learn the hard way! Honestly, I'm super thankful for those moments because I learned *so* much and overcame more by climbing over those hills. Without hardships, I would be naive. Maybe even vanilla, bland, or boring. Not that having an easy, simple life makes you ordinary, but it was never for me. I knew I needed an adventure, some sort of trial to taste what it was like to fail and get back up again. If I hadn't gone through the mud, I'd have no story to tell. I would be lost trying to find meaning. My purpose was to get wrecked in the face a few times and live to share it. So think of it like this: if you win, great; if you lose, you learn a lesson, but you didn't fail. Get the hell back up or get lost in the dust. If you dwell on your shortcomings, you will become a product of them. Your failures will become a life theme. Let's put our power in humility so we can create a story for our life that is extraordinary.

My desire for adventure hurtled me toward self-destruction and self-loathing. That journey went a little something like this: I was lonely and depressed. It felt agonizing to be alone and stuck in my own head. I could not bear silence because it left me to face the inner noise. My trying to shut out the noise caused heavy drinking, poor relationships, and an overall lack of care for my life and for others. I was turned off, tuned out. Today didn't matter and neither did tomorrow. I allowed myself to become a product of my low self-esteem. My life motto was, "My life sucks." How selfish.

My self-pity was rooted in pride. But by the grace of God, my heart awoke from its prideful slumber. It was slow in the beginning. My understanding of pride started like a few drops of rain here and there. Then it became a drizzle. Eventually, it poured. I was drenched—so deep in the storm, I couldn't avoid it if I tried. Now when I look back, I see my journey was led by humility all along. Even when I wasn't always aware of its presence, humility was taking the lead and many amazing things were happening.

Now I have meaning and real joy. Not fleeting joy that came from a night of drinking. I have people in my life who truly love me for me. I am part of the world of entrepreneurship, a world I never would've dreamed I was meant for with my previous mentality. Doors were flung open, and I realized I was capable of anything. Pride was stopping me all along.

That pride was so hidden because I didn't know certain things I did were even prideful. I wasn't aware that judgment, selfishness, and short-temperedness were manifestations of straight-up pride! Some people go their whole lives without seeing pride for what it is. How will you fix it if you don't even see it? That's why I'm so excited to be writing about this. I hope it brings an eye-opening moment to at least one reader. If humility can start a chain reaction of awakenings in someone else like it did for me, then writing this book was well worth it.

You know that feeling when your power goes off during a summer storm? You feel so hopeless. You feel like you can't believe how much you depend on your sweet electricity. The house gets hot. You can't do your usual daily tasks. Comfortable living is no more. It's kind of depressing. But then . . . your power comes back. Oh, glorious day! You can't believe how much you missed it. You're so happy to take a hot shower that you could kiss the bathtub! You're so thankful. You decide to never take electricity for granted again. You see and feel it for the blessing it is.

That's what humility feels like. I have it every day. I feel immense gratitude that I'm not where I used to be. It's hard to believe that life can be so wonderful. That all of *this* is mine. I sometimes can't believe this joy is real. I want that same joy for everyone. I want everyone to come to the same epiphany. But before I show you what it takes, decide right now that you will be open to hearing this information without judgment. Cast your pride aside, and read this book as if it's true. Decide that this book can help you. That you will try to find something in here that can be applied or that can be harnessed. You need to consciously decide to listen to what I'm going to say. You need to decide that this applies to you, that you aren't above what I'm about to talk about. This is the first step toward humility. Toward casting your ego aside. Maybe your heart is already an open slate ready to receive. If it is, I applaud you! We need more of you in our world.

It's human nature to look for what we don't like in something. We're always looking to debunk. Hello! That was me when I read books from self-help gurus. They can often feel fluffy AF and unattainable.

I have not reached maximum enlightenment, sitting on a cloud of pure happiness. I'm still walking down the gravel path, dirt on my face, clothes battered, and skin peeling from the molten-hot sun. Just kidding. Still, it's an accurate description of this inner walk I'm taking.

My point is to take something from this book. Something, anything! I bet you'll continue to beat yourself up until you fix some of this stuff. There is so much hurt that needs to come out and be dealt with. There is bitterness; there is competitiveness. Get it all out. Be done with it. Open up your heart to what I'm going to say, or live the rest of your life in the shadow of pride. Your choice.

If nothing else, at least take a good look at yourself. Most people don't even see the fruit of pride in their life, much less its roots. Recognize it. Look at it. If you don't see it, you can't begin to work on it.

Just don't let this book make you "high and mighty." That is the opposite of its intent. When I first recognized what pride was, I started to notice it in other people and took it upon myself to confront them: "Hey, you've got a pride problem there. Be humble." Not a good move. First off, they were not ready to receive a humility lesson. Second, it was not my place to give one. Turns out, telling someone to be humble is not a humble thing to do. Pointing out other people's flaws is never okay; it's not our place if they do not ask. So do not go around with a "holier than thou" mentality once you've finished this book, preaching at people about why they should change.

Another thing I want to prepare you for—I will be name-dropping my man Jesus Christ. If you are not a person of faith, please do not let that deter you from reading this book. Its message is valuable no matter who you are or what you believe. Humility works for *everyone*. This is not a religious book, but in telling my story, I refer to God. I wouldn't be able to tell you about my trials without including him, because that is my truth. Feel free to replace "God" with whatever you believe. I promise humility works whether you are a believer, an agnostic, or a follower of the Flying Spaghetti Monster.

Also, another disclaimer. I curse a little. I know, maybe it seems a little un-Godlike. Maybe it is. But, my friend, I'm writing for you like I'm talking to a friend. I want to be myself when I tell you about my life. I'm not a robot; I'm using my real voice while writing. I'm not going to pretend I don't say "Oh shit!" a couple of times a day. That said, I have back-and-forth feelings about "bad words." I have come to accept that context matters most. Saying "I had a shitty day" describes how your day went and doesn't hurt anyone's feelings. Saying "that girl looks like shit on a stick" is mean and does hurt someone's feelings.

So let's get to it. Be open to feeling conviction. Be open to realizing you were wrong. Be open to being okay with feeling shame when you hurt someone else. Let these realizations surface. Let all the darkness come to the light and lay it bare before you. Stare at it. Then burn it, throw the ashes in the air, and start flying.

CHAPTER 1

WHEN I WAS NOT HUMBLE

So let me talk about the dark ages in my life. I was a mess. A defensive ego. Full of pride. You couldn't tell me what to do without making me feel controlled or attacked. At the time, I was waitressing at a barbecue joint. Anytime another nineteen-year-old waitress rolled her eyes because I asked a question they thought was obvious or a customer tore me apart because we ran out of pulled pork, it ruined me. I resented their existence for *years*. How—*how*—could I be treated so unfairly? I was just trying my best. If you've ever worked in the service industry, you know how it feels to be the punching bag for people's anger.

I later realized that some people are just mean. They seem to think it's okay to lash out because a coworker doesn't do the job exactly as they would or because they didn't get what they wanted. The world is unfair. The way you deal with this unfairness is up to you. Me? I was just mad all the time. I started questioning *anything* a person of authority said to me. Their rules and restrictions often made no sense, so I pushed back. Even before being mistreated as a waitress, I had a rebellious streak. At the ripe age of twelve, I buzzed off the sides of my hair and gave myself a Mohawk. After my parents told me not to, of course. At thirteen, I gave myself a jailhouse wrist tattoo with a sewing needle and ink from a ballpoint pen. I still have it to this day. (Very unsafe and unsanitary, so I recommend *not* doing this, ever.)

At age fifteen, I entered my first real relationship with a man who was about twenty-three years old. He was clearly too old to be dating a girl my age. He pitted me against my parents and manipulated me into staying with him for as long as I did, which was way too long for someone eight years his junior. He threatened me whenever I tried to break us up. Although I did escape that relationship, the emotional abuse was everlasting. (Also, when your fifteen-year-old girlfriend is outgrowing her adult boyfriend, maybe it's a sign, dude.)

At sixteen, I gave my parents so much hell that they let me move out. I couch surfed at different friends' houses for a few years. During eleventh grade, I dropped out of high school, partied, drank every night, and drove black-out drunk so many times, I have no idea how I didn't get into a car accident or get a DUI.

I was an absolute mess. A mess! Despite my protests, my parents forced me to go to church three times a week—Sunday morning service, Sunday evening youth group, Wednesday night service. I *hated* it. And I let my parents know. All Sunday afternoon, I sulked in my bedroom and listened to the Misfits and other punk rock bands. For church, I wore all black to embarrass my conservative parents in front of their friends. Despite my behavior, I did believe in God, but I resented the fact that my parents wanted me to "do Christianity" *their* way. I also disliked how fake-happy everyone seemed, how bland and vanilla it all felt. The hugging, the singing, the preaching. Smiles and prayers seemed rehearsed. Many probably were. Church is a business, after all. The pastor has to come up with a message every week. Still, how could I be the only one who wanted to be my true self at church? It just felt so fake to be . . . fake.

It took having my first child to realize my parents tried their best. They thought attending church would somehow lead me down a safer path. I now understand something about church and religion in general: churches are made by imperfect humans. Yes, believers might try to follow a perfect God, but the humans who build and run churches are still sinners. Some churches so poorly convey God's message, they turn born-again Christians away from Jesus. Yikes!

People make mistakes, even people who claim to represent God. The church disappointed me because I had unrealistic expectations. Only God can bring me joy. I cannot depend on a person or a church to fill that need. Yes, it helps to have a community of people who support you, which I did, but one can't expect imperfect humans to always portray God's love. Pride tells us we deserve to be treated a certain way, and if we aren't, we're entitled to feel bitter and unforgiving. I've seen such idealistic expectations drive other people out of Christianity, never to return.

We need to learn humility; our eternal fate depends on it. So do our human relationships. We should expect humans to fall short of our expectations. We all want our parents, siblings, spouses, friends, and coworkers to treat us a certain way, yet if we don't also realize they *will* let us down at some point, we're setting ourselves up for exaggerated disappointment. So release those expectations. Assume the people you love and respect won't always treat you the way you want to be treated. And decide now that when they hurt you—*when*, not *if*—give them grace. Show mercy. Put yourself in their shoes. Did they really intend to betray you? Let's be real. We humans tend to let emotions get the better of us. We act out, sometimes lash out, in frustration that has little to do with the person in front of us. But that's who we hurt. Whether we mean it or not. If we all simply accept we do this, we'd be a lot nicer to each other.

This is why we need a relationship with God. Or whatever you want to call it—the universe, yourself, a higher power, etc. Once you find inner peace outside human relationships, you can truly enjoy them.

I promise, this chapter is the only one that talks about God this much. This is not a Bible study. My friends are reading this book. They don't all believe in Jesus. I feel like God took me on this humility journey so I can share his message without freaking people the hell out. I accept and love everyone. All people have a place at my table. I give a shit about you no matter what. Come to me however you are. The more broken the better. That's why I don't spend all my time pitching Jesus. The way you sell something is to live it. For my faith, that means to just be a good friend. Be reliable. Listen. Care. Show kindness. That is how you influence.

CHAPTER 2

WHEN PRIDE FIRST REVEALED ITSELF

During my teenage rebellion phase, my mom gave me a book by Rick Joyner, some dude known for "edgy" Christianity. I was never a big reader. Between getting drunk every night and acting like a psycho, where would I find the time? I have no idea what compelled me to read the book other than the fact that my whisper of a conscience told me I was acting like a dirt human.

The book is *The Final Quest*, an allegory of the battle between good and evil. It shook me. Like when you see a cool outfit, try it on, look in the mirror, and lurch back in horror that you could ever look so uncool. That was me. That was my pride. In the book, a character called Wisdom tells the protagonist that, paraphrasing here, "Pride is the sneakiest of enemies." Pride. An enemy. The toughest to spot and hardest to kill.

For the first time in my life, I acknowledged pride as wrong. I never considered myself prideful until I read that line about pride. I always thought proud people were the girls who took a million selfies, scoffed at people who couldn't afford their clothes, and flipped their hair every five seconds.

I wondered how come I had never considered myself an egotistical person. Yet I was. Did adults fall prey to pride as I had? I later realized most adults do. As I grew up, I saw thirty- and even forty-somethings living wild like I had as a teenager. And let me tell ya . . . they're miserable. Anger, parties, alcohol. Anger, parties, alcohol. Over and over. I did *not* want to be miserable my whole life.

Did realizing I had an ego issue make me change? Nope. Funny how that works. My pride was wrestled out of my clenched, bloody fingers when I got pregnant, got married, and had the baby, all within a year. Luckily, I got married to the best man in the world for me. Once we had our son, shit got real. I mean *real* real. First of all, becoming a mom is a humbling experience. Having your goods wide open for everyone to see is as vulnerable as it gets. Also, nobody ever told me there would be so much blood during childbirth. I was mortified. And in love. A love I cannot explain. It made me—someone who never, ever wanted kids—think a baby was cute.

I realized that nothing in this life mattered except the love I had to give. I was so small compared to the big, important person I once thought I was. At home recovering with my newborn, I hit a wall of shame for all the wrong I had done, all the hurt I caused. I went from immature girl to gentle, thoughtful woman. Literally overnight. Crazy.

With this divine clarity came a long period of loneliness. I fell into a deep depression, probably triggered by my first pregnancy.

CHAPTER 3

HOW HUMILITY GREW MY BUSINESS

I said this book wasn't a memoir, so you're probably wondering why I'm telling my story. It all ties together—promise. I cannot explain how I learned humility without the events that taught me. Perhaps you'll even find them relatable.

So there I was. Lying low in our apartment complex of crackheads hollering at me anytime I went outside. Toddlers ran around with no adult supervision. I wasn't active on social media and had no friends. I was still in shock from pushing a baby out of my body, but I was bored. Exhausted. Restless.

My husband worked tireless hours as a sheriff's deputy, and I was alone at home crying every day because I couldn't take it. They don't pay cops nearly enough. My husband's paychecks hardly paid our bills. It was a humble way of living, and I still told myself every day how thankful I was. Everything was a blessing. Every meal, every conversation with a new friend, every rare date night. Even those paychecks.

Something pulled at my heart. Something different. Something I was meant to do.

A close friend growing up was a talented photographer. I was her muse. As teenagers, we ventured into abandoned buildings with a suitcase of random clothes. I swung from ropes while modeling for her, climbed the trees outside wearing absurd outfits, and once got covered in monstrous beetles because I changed in a bush behind a factory.

As I watched my friend edit photos of me, I told myself I could do this too. One day, I would buy a camera. One day. It was way too expensive a dream for a teenager awful at saving money. So I slept on it. For years.

I had never invested in a camera because of the price. I was always worried about spending the extra money, only to realize it was another venture I got bored of, sucked at, or could not finish. As a stay-at-home mom, wasting money was not an option for my family, but stay-at-home motherhood gave me too much time alone with my thoughts. The few pleasant ones were memories of me and my photo buddy. Now was as good a time as any to say yes to myself. We took the risk, and my supportive husband, who just wanted me to be happy, opened up a new credit card to get me my first camera.

As soon as I decided which camera I wanted, my heart fluttered. I could hardly sleep the first week I had it. Every day, I took more pictures than the day before. I watched hours-long editing tutorials. The obsession continued for weeks, then months. I took photos of anything and anyone in our apartment complex who consented. I had no expectation of making money, much less getting good enough to ask for it. My only goal was to have something I could call my own.

Then a neighbor texted me.

Hey Jessica. So I heard you do photography. I'd like to try and get a family picture. My budget is only twenty. But could you maybe take a couple of photos for that?

I could not believe the win. Someone wanted to pay me for my passion? No self-help guru needed to tell me how special that is. Especially since I felt like paying *her* twenty dollars for asking me. You know that Bible verse about not despising small beginnings? A little voice told me to look it up, and I did. I hadn't yet realized—as I snapped, edited, and printed my first photo session—that those twenty bucks marked my humble foray into an adventure of a lifetime.

My neighbor introduced me to a friend, who offered me fifty dollars for a family photo shoot. Wow . . . a whole half a hundred. Unreal. A half-dozen more referrals from these first two customers, and I paid off the camera. Then I turned around and bought my *dream* camera, similar to the one my friend used during our wild photo shoots.

Despite my unreasonably low expectations, the money kept coming—and growing. I thanked God through tears the night I realized I'd made my first $1,000 as a professional photographer. Yep, I'd turned pro. That's what happens when you get paid. Technically, that first twenty dollars qualified me for the title as much as my first $2,000 wedding, which came within my first couple years in business. The whole time, I felt so lucky. Even to this day, when I make one hundred dollars, I'm grateful. Every win is a reward from God for my finally giving up my pride.

If I had dabbled with photography myself as a teenager, it would have been for all the wrong reasons. I probably would not have met my husband or had our children. I needed to endure a season of loneliness and reflect on my pride in my heart.

That doesn't mean I stayed perfect. Pride is persistent. As the checks got bigger, so did my ego. I was trying so hard to make money that I had wrapped my pride up in it. I forgot to be thankful that I even got to do what I loved at all. I forgot all the pain I felt as a depressed, lonely soul that I said "Woe is me!" all over again.

Within a few years, I stopped saying thank-you for small projects and started living in fear. *What if this wedding season isn't as busy as last year's? Or people for whatever reason decide to move in together rather than get married? And don't have cute little kids who need their pictures taken every year?*

All pride disguised as worry. Release the pride, relieve the anxiety. That's what I did. In the same way I watched educational videos to learn photography fundamentals, I took online personal finance and business budgeting bookkeeping. All to learn the humble way to manage my money, earn more, and make it stretch as far as possible. Through those lessons, I learned how to be thankful again. I also learned a lot about happiness—how joy, self-awareness, patience, gratitude, and a pile of other things come with humility. A humble spirit is this big outer circle with all these desirable feelings inside. If you are humble, you are self-aware. If you are humble, you are grateful. If you are humble, you have joy. I could go on and on.

I failed at humility over and over in my business. I also failed in the business itself. A stupid editing mistake got a customer irate. Trying to find parking in Downtown Miami with no luck had me late to a session and made my client very unhappy. Little shit like that. It adds up.

What sets humble people apart is the recognition that we are not entitled to 100 percent success. After failure, many who never get back up again cannot get over the shock of getting punched by life in the first place. Ego cannot believe it when something doesn't go its way. Me? I fell, got back up, let myself get punched again like a dummy, and rose all over again. Each time I checked my pride, learned a valuable lesson, and changed course. Humility won't let you get comfortable in one place. Humility simply tells you what doesn't work anymore so you can move on and grow. And humility is listening.

I finally started to love the process more than the money I was making. Because the journey taught me not only how to earn more money but how to keep it so I could provide a comfortable, full life for my family. *That* is what I overlooked when ego drove me.

Now when I look at other successful entrepreneurs, they all have one trait in common—humility. Entrepreneurs who "make it" fail, get back up, fail, and get back up over and over until they win. It might be years of blood, sweat, and tears until they finally win.

Success is more than money. Money is just paper. It's not revenue most entrepreneurs chase. It's happiness. I often see entrepreneurs not want money necessarily for their own benefit but so they can finally be in a position to better the world around them. Whether it's through teaching what they've learned, giving to charities, helping out single parents, or buying their own parents a home. They often know what it was once like to struggle.

I don't think most entrepreneurs realize how self-aware they are, much less realize how they're practicing humility. Consider the mental and emotional self-growth required to risk everything and keep it all "on the table" every day. When we see we're wrong, we change course. Being in business means you have no choice. You cannot blame the market, the competitor, or the customer. Well, you can, but you won't make any money doing that. Successful entrepreneurs always take full responsibility for their business failures, regroup, and get back up after a stomping. That's humility.

Among aspiring entrepreneurs, I often see "sassiness" and a "screw you, I'm going to do and say what I want and not care what others think" attitude glorified. Most who act that way never start a business. Those of us who do get a business off the ground care what others think. Hello, we have to. Ever heard of these people called customers?

All said and done, to the humble entrepreneur, there is winning, and there is learning valuable lessons. Losing does not exist. No losses, only lessons.

CHAPTER 4

WHY YOUR WHY ISN'T ABOUT YOU

Why do you want to make money, Jessica? After all, it's not the green rectangular piece of paper I'm after; it's the end goal that I seek. For me personally, I want to finance a better lifestyle for me and my family so we can go on memorable adventures together and not feel constricted by financial obligations. I would like to be able to have a seafood feast every once in a while and not feel guilty because it's a little pricey. I would like to be able to fund my children's passions so they can find what they love.

My why is also living in a place that feels like home. It's going on fun adventures with my husband and kids. It's throwing parties and hosting Thanksgiving and Christmas. That's why I work. I needed to discover my true aspirations so I could stop chasing money and start chasing a life that brings me joy. The life I wanted includes enough financial stability to be present in my life and lend a helping hand to those around me.

It's not selfish to want money in your life. Money is simply a means to an end. It helps us finance a life that is ideal. The more money good people have, the more resources they have to help the world with. So if you think you're a good person, you can put money to use and make the world a better place. Even if it starts in your home.

If you are looking to start a business or grow your finances just so you can look cool, but you really don't have any sort of sentimental goal, finding motivation might wear off quickly. (Side note: If money is a hard topic for you, and wanting it seems to go against everything you know about being humble, I suggest reading *The Science of Getting Rich* and *You Are a Badass at Making Money*.)

Your *why* needs to include a bigger picture that evokes lasting inspiration. When you think of joy, what comes to mind? Who is next to you? What things are you doing with the people you love that bring you joy? A *why* is so much deeper than outward appearances. I believe we all have a deep inner mission that's not just based on gaining money or living a popular lifestyle. The pure *why* we're all born with is actually a deep-rooted desire to make the world a better place and feel whole. The way a humble person feels whole is by helping others. Also, we could argue that it's really the only way to feel whole. People who do things out of pride and selfishness are not whole. They're using negative means to fill a void that only humility can fill. Something about serving others is spiritual. Heavenly. The amount of power that goes out into the world when we do something with no intention of receiving anything back . . . it's eternal.

We cannot influence the world in a healthy way until we ourselves are healthy. Be aware of your intentions. Find your *why*, the real one. Not the ego-driven one, the "make the world a better place" one. Once you're aware of why it's important to serve the world with your talents, you will have so much more peace in taking risks. You will realize how it's essentially a disservice to the world if you do not attempt to make the world a better place with your talents.

And that's why your *why* is never about you. For years, I wanted to help others to make myself feel good. I even did overseas mission work in Guatemala. My hands might have been in the right place, but the rest of me was not. I served for *my* sake. How did I come up with the sham of an ideal? Oh right—I was prideful AF. It was all about me, always. Even when I acted like I wanted to live a selfless kumbaya Christian lifestyle. I needed to sit down, stay put, and be humble.

Helping those less fortunate is still on my mind and in my heart. Yet I have no agenda, no big plans, no "How can I make myself feel good?" mission trips planned. I simply give as I feel God leads. Sometimes it's donating money. Other times, it's giving an afternoon or a week to a cause. Humility responds to need. Ego maps a path, one where the glory is all yours in the end.

Humility is when you realize you were spared the consequences you earned because of egotistical acts that led you astray. This kind of humility is a blessing beyond understanding.

CHAPTER 5

3X GENEROSITY

Generosity is quite simply the act of being generous. Most people are told from infancy that sharing is caring. Indeed that statement is correct. You heard it here, folks. That's all for today. Lesson learned. C'ya never!

Just kidding. There is more to discover about generosity, its close sister humility, and how the two work their magic to bless you beyond your wildest ambitions. Let's start with the fact that generosity takes three forms:

1. **Literal generosity**: The act of giving something physical or of value.
2. **Service generosity**: Acts of service and being helpful.
3. **Emotional generosity**: Being deeply empathetic and truly wanting to lift up someone and make them feel good.

With gratitude comes generosity. Otherwise you have neither. You can say you are thankful, but damn, dude, if you don't show it, I don't know if you're all that thankful. Those who are grateful not only feel it, they show it. Giving is the natural response to receiving. And

I don't mean giving in order to get more. Give selflessly. Give anonymously. Give with no expectation of ever receiving in return. This is humility. This is empathy.

You probably know all about literal generosity and service generosity. I imagine you've given to a charity or volunteered your time for a good cause. Perhaps the hardest form of generosity is emotional. It's when we feel another person's need. We see their plight. The struggle is real. We relate. So we give. Our money, our food, our stuff, our time, our love. Empathy followed by generosity. I say this as someone with an empathy problem. Now, I'm not some monster who feels nothing for anyone. I love those around me. But I've often found myself uninterested in hearing people's problems. I've brushed them off and pretended to listen. Or given terrible, unsolicited advice. Because I just didn't care about focusing on someone else's emotions. So selfish.

Every day, I decide to choose empathy. The first few decisions looked . . . rough. When I realized I needed to fix my empathy issue, I did what I thought people do when they listen. Look you in the eye, ask questions, nod a lot. All to pretend I was listening. But when you pretend to hear, you don't listen. To their pain points. What they need you to solve. How they want your help and when. This must have been apparent. I'm a bad faker and also terrible at sales.

Once I became an emotional listener, I realized it was never about selling. Listening is about showing empathy and fulfilling my clients' desires reliably. How could I serve them if I did not hear what they really wanted? Early in my business, I pitched my services using fancy words neither of us understood but I assumed would make me sound qualified. When I learned how to make every client conversation about them and not me, about making *them* happy, not making *me* money, my business broke through every growth barrier I perceived, from how many clients wanted to hire me at any given time to how much they were willing to pay to how much bacon I brought home at the end of the month. I know that sounds generic. A lot of business owners might think they're putting customers first, but most aren't. You have to break out of the confines of traditional business practices and get a little uncomfortable to feel true empathy for your customers.

Listening with empathy *is* generosity. Because the person speaking feels the attention you're giving. Take my husband, for instance. God bless that man who has to put up with me. He's the reason I realized I had a listening problem. One day, he looked me dead in the face and told me everything he says goes in one ear and out the other.

"I can literally see my words leaving the other ear" were his exact words. "When I'm talking, it's like your brain just shuts off and tunes me out."

Where's the lie, though? My husband would remind me of an appointment every day for a week, but when the time rolled around, I literally had no idea what he was talking about. That's wrong. When he generously listens to me and remembers what I consider important, failing to reciprocate shows I'm selfish, ungrateful, and immature. I could have made excuses. I sure had them. I was busy with one baby, then two, and a business makes three. Nope. I owned up and changed.

Did I go from zoned out to tuned in 100 percent of the time? Mama brain makes that impossible. So I kept a notepad and calendar on hand at all times. Even if I had a hard time remembering, I was always looking at my calendar. I knew that if I wrote something down there, I would remember it. I'm a full-blown adult—my husband should expect to count on me. In marriage, that's how you show love and gratitude. You follow through. You become generous within yourself and outside yourself. My husband won't know I'm thankful for him if I can't offer the bare-minimum spouse.

It's not like generosity is a chore. Giving makes you feel so damn good. Just this week was my niece's second birthday party. The night before, I spent far too long at Target trying to pick the perfect gift. I ended up with princess-themed play makeup, adorable sunglasses, and some wall-hanging decor. I couldn't wait for her to see her gifts. She would light up. Once we finally got to her presents, she opened mine first and, of course, loved them. We pretended to put on the lipstick, blush, and eye shadow.

Reflecting on my niece's birthday, I question why I was so excited to give her presents. She's two. She wasn't even aware of what a birthday is. She's not able to give back in any material way. Yet making her special day all the brighter made me feel the greatest. I gained more through that interaction than I could have ever given that tiny tot.

The point is generosity is never wasted, even if the recipient doesn't comprehend it or even abuses it. I have this rule: Anytime I see a homeless person, if I have something to give, I give it to them. Even if they look drugged out. Who knows their story? Maybe they haven't eaten in days because they were on a bender and need food. Maybe they have kids who are also hungry and need food. Maybe they're mentally ill or have PTSD. Or maybe they're addicts and will buy more drugs. Even if that's the case, you have uncovered something they now have to face should they lie to you about why they need money. Sometimes that uncovering will reveal hope they so badly need; sometimes your gift will suppress it. Either way, your effort was gracious and glorious.

It is our sacred duty to be generous even when we don't know how the other person will respond. Now, don't let this be confused with giving money to anyone and everyone. Don't allow yourself to be cheated out of your money by family and friends because you think giving to anyone who asks is okay. If certain people have made a habit of taking from you, refuse to be a victim of their greed one more day. If you have a sibling who is always borrowing money, swearing to pay it back, but never following through, protect yourself. There are other ways to give to such people. Perhaps they need your prayers more than anything.

But giving freely to the homeless and needy is such a high form of generosity. It is taught in many religious doctrines that it's our duty to give, and there is a big reason for it. You are not only giving to someone in need but to a complete stranger you might never see again and who will never reciprocate. You are giving just to give. Because you know it's right. And because it makes the world a better place.

One time in New York City, I saw a street beggar being ignored by everyone walking past. I stopped and gave anyway. Someone next to me was about to walk by but paused their swift walk and gave money to the homeless man. Simply because he saw *me* do it.

When I practice giving—attention, time, or money—I receive so much back. Sometimes it's a clear and peaceful heart. Would you love to be happy? Content? Full of joy and at peace?

Then give. And you shall receive.

CHAPTER 6

DO YOU REALLY DESERVE THAT?

"I deserve that."

I hate that phrase. Think about it. Why do you deserve it, truly? What about it do you deserve? When you were born, did you receive a certificate with a list of entitlements you deserve? When we're born, we are not guaranteed anything. Except death, taxes, and a Social Security number, if you're born in the United States. We aren't guaranteed food, water, shelter, good parents, good friends, a raise at our job, kids who behave. I could go on. We don't even have guarantees about our own lives. Life is so unpredictable that at any moment, it can be taken from you. That's how we know we were not born to deserve anything.

The expectation that we deserve something causes great disappointment, then bitterness when we don't get it. *But I deserved this! I worked so hard, and Susy has been so lazy in this company. Everyone sees it. How could she get moved to management and not me? I've even been here longer, and I love my job* way *more! I deserved this, I earned this!*

If you believe you deserve a reward, congratulations. You are now disqualified from it. That might boggle your brain.

You go, girl! You worked so hard, you deserve a vacay! Yas, queen!

Yeah, that's a hard no from me. Nobody in world history ever deserved a vacation. In other countries, people work sixteen hours a day, seven days a week to be able to feed their families. They know they will never get a vacation for their hard work. Not even food is guaranteed. They are 100 percent right.

What about paychecks? Paid time off? Compliments you've earned? These are exactly that—rewards you've *earned*. Still, you haven't earned something if you haven't received it yet. Once you receive what you've earned, then you can say, "I earned this!" Because you did. It's there in front of you. Earning is an action followed by a result. Deserving is an attitude followed by whining if you don't receive what you wanted.

That said, I don't think pep-talking yourself with *I deserve this, I worked hard* is wrong. Sure, I let "I deserve it" slip out every so often. But when "I deserve it because I want it so I must have it" becomes a mentality, no matter how much you think it's owed to you, it never is. It's self-manipulation that keeps you from putting in the effort to earn it instead.

That's why you see the word "deserve" abused every day in politics. "The people deserve _____." Really, though? Do they? At what point in life were the people appointed this guarantee and by whom? What we think we deserve, we often base on what other people tell us we do. How can you expect to receive something based on what an imperfect human says? How are we to know what we deserve? Also, who gets to decide when we finally get what we deserve? Do we? I think I deserve that promotion, but Susy is convinced she does. Who's right? Who decides?

Now imagine the opposite situation. You might think you don't deserve something great you received. Let's say someone randomly gifts you $500. You have no idea who. You've never given anyone that much money or given the equivalent monetary value as a gift. But you have it now. No, you were not born deserving this money, but you have received it. Someone somewhere decided it should be yours. Can you really say you *deserved* that gift?

See, the more we dissect "deserve," the deeper we find ourselves lost in an empty term. It means nothing because it can mean anything. There is no law of nature or ultimate measure to confirm you are ready to receive what you deserve. Our hearts are so hardened that we assume everything is about us. In reality, if you do not receive what you thought was yours, then it's not yours, and nobody owes you. But if you do receive it, tell yourself, *I received this because I earned it.*

We will burn out if we have rigid expectations for what the world owes us, how people should treat us, or how things should run. Expectations tie in with patience and forgiveness. Being humble means considering the big picture before yourself. If traffic is *so* slow, you're about to be late, and you curse the drivers around you, you have shown no patience. You have unreasonable expectations. You're driving a man-made car on a man-made road going to a man-made place. I emphasize "man-made" because we don't realize how arbitrary and imperfect all these are and how ridiculous it is to expect perfection from a system built by humans. Chillax. Even if you don't get there in time or don't make it at all, relax. Forgive. Fate does not owe you or anyone else clear roads. It does not owe you a promotion. Nor does the world owe you a perfect tropical island vacation.

When you go through life with no expectation of how things should play out, you experience the lasting inner peace you've always desired. You will be *free*. Your heart will run through tall grass blowing in the breeze below a glistening golden-hour sunset and clear skies. Pure joy!

This also applies to people treating you badly. Sure, you've been a great friend, you're as nice to everyone as you can be, and you truly try! But that same person puts you down whenever you see them. Or take your ex baby daddy, who hauls you in front of a judge to try to get full custody of the beloved child you birthed.

I don't deserve this! Hello. The world is cruel. There are no limits to the evil that can happen. The one thing we're guaranteed is that good and bad happen to us, no matter what. The way we deal with them is how we're measured when we meet God. He doesn't care if anybody sees it; it doesn't need to be between you and the world. It's between you and God. Humility is about the state of your heart when nobody sees what happened. It's about deciding to love and forgive when nobody knows you did. Take responsibility for your emotions. Don't steal your own joy.

Another "deserve" alternative besides "earn" is "worth," as in, "I am worthy of this." I looked up the definition of "earn," and it said, "to make worthy of or obtain for." I love this because the Bible states we're worthy of many wonderful blessings, including the love of God when we do not deserve it. Being worthy takes the expectation of deserving off the table. Yes, you're worthy of a raise; you're a hard worker. You may not have gotten it, though, and that's okay because you're worthy of many other rewards as well. Faith and patience will bring you something else beyond what you dreamed. Sometimes the better, more amazing thing is peace and contentment within your soul. It's giving to the poor or loving God so much your heart overflows.

Your blessing might not be monetary. Life is fleeting. Cash and possessions do not represent how worthy your life is. That is humility—accepting that you might be a millionaire, or you might live in poverty picking up trash off the side of the road for a living.

Either way, I am content. I am free. I am grateful for being worthy of breathing. Humility is okay with either outcome.

I'm also a big believer in personal and professional growth. So when I say be okay with both outcomes, I don't mean remain stationary and keep picking up trash because you don't think you're capable of bigger or better. Yes, be grateful for what you have, but consider it a place in passing. Your success has no bounds. Do not stay stagnant for the sake of humility. "Look how low I am. I'm so poor and helpless and humble" is pride talking. You can be humble and also be incredibly wealthy. But never feel ashamed if you tried your hardest and picking up trash is the only gig you can get. Bring your light to the world any way you can. If that means saying hi to every person on your trash route, meeting them with smiles and compliments, then yes!

Humility is *always* grateful. Even during traumatic events. Let's say you get hit by a car, and you get your leg pinned. Next thing you know, you wake up in a hospital, and your leg is gone. The surgeon had to amputate because someone decided to drink and drive. This extreme example shows my point. The only expectation we should have of life is that breakthroughs and tragedies can happen to anyone at any time.

It's awful to endure hardship, I know. It's happening. It's here. Now what? Mourning is okay. Fear and sadness are okay. I imagine it's quite traumatic to wake up with a limb missing. But finding someone to blame or venting anger because something bad happened that you didn't deserve is not okay. Yes, of course, the drunk driver made a choice that affected your life forever. But where is your heart? Do bad things happening give you the go-ahead to be bitter and unforgiving? You cannot blame that person for ruining your life. Once the deed is done, the only person ruining your life . . . is you. You're the thief of your own joy, the chains keeping you captive. You are literally not even born with the expectation that your limbs are owed to you for the rest of your life. You aren't even given the promise of your own life. Billions of babies throughout history never made it out of the womb. Bless those mothers who have to endure the loss of a child. Even now, you who are reading this . . . you. Are. Still. Breathing. How awesome is that?

I in no way want to diminish the losses you have experienced. I cannot imagine going through the sudden loss of a loved one or some other tragedy like the ones that make headlines worldwide every day. I don't know what it's like to starve or to feel terrified of where I live. But I do know there are people who are starving, who have been brutalized, who have never been given a chance but are *much* more grateful and humble than I am. That's on me.

As I said, I'm *not* perfect. A few days ago, after booking some weddings and thinking about how many goals I killed this year, I said out loud, "I'm rich, bitch!" Which is not even close to true, yet I was stoked on making money because making money is great.

Yeah, that's what not to do. It's okay to celebrate yourself, but probably not that way. Pat yourself on the back. Take yourself out to a nice dinner after a big sale. Tell your spouse about what you accomplished. Feel proud. Just don't brag. Especially don't yell "I'm rich, bitch!" in your house while you're dressed in an old XXL T-shirt with makeup smeared around your eyes like a freak. Not a hot look.

Also, don't put yourself down when you're given recognition for your success. Receive that compliment with an open heart. You are worthy of it and have earned it! Being humble is not saying, "Oh no, I don't want to take the credit at all. It has nothing to do with me." Humility is gratitude for praise. If other people helped, of course spread the love and share the praise. To give you must also be open to receiving. Even if the praise is from your spouse, let it water the garden of your heart. Give back what you have been given anytime you get a chance. Flower the gardens of others.

CHAPTER 7

THE KARDASHIAN COMPLEX

How you talk about the Kardashians says a lot about you. This family has been long judged in so many ways. I have heard every nasty comment you can imagine about these women. I have heard them called every name in the book, and they are met with eye rolls, scoffs, and negative words.

I use the Kardashians as an example because they're targeted so often, but this applies to any rich or famous person. Hurtful words and uninformed judgments of strangers and celebrities reveals nastiness in our hearts. Mob mentality tells us it's okay to hate them because they are—we assume—selfish, materialistic, dumb, untalented, etc.

Those in need are easy to love because they are easy to pity. The privileged are not. But our goodness is based not on how we treat the easy to love but how we treat those who are *not*. Humility loves those who may not deserve your love. Humility loves people who think they're better than you. Humility loves those who are rich beyond words. It loves those who hurt others and those who make bad choices. Everyone.

Where is your heart for people you don't like? The people who don't like you? Love them. Show grace and have mercy. We are all fragile humans. We are products of the world in which we grew up. We make good and bad choices. It's not okay for us to decide who is not worthy of love because of their sins. Because "sin" is subjective. Just ask a Baptist Christian to compare notes with a Roman Catholic. Often, "sin" consists of breaking imperfect rules made by imperfect humans. Intuition alone cannot be trusted to cast pure and right judgment onto these people. It's not okay to assume a rich person is both rich and selfish. The fact you think you're more righteous than the Kardashians or Biebers proves you are not. You're far beneath them. We are all built to be worthy of the same love. In fact, lack of love is probably what creates all these people you don't like anyway.

How much time do we waste thinking about what we *don't* like about someone rather than what we do? We must train our hearts to recognize the goodness in someone first. I get it, though—it's just about impossible to feel compassion for someone who did unspeakable deeds like murder. Crimes against children ruin me. Such people might not seem to deserve love, mercy, or even their own life.

We're quick to assume they're evil, soulless monsters who must be treated as such. But we must also love them and with urgency. I 100 percent believe lack of real love at some point in these people's lives made their once warm hearts go cold. Remember, we were all babies once, craving genuine love. I have mercy for the worst of the worst because they were once innocent children. That child is always in there. Often, people turn into predators because they're victims of unspeakable abuse themselves.

Love does not mean we make excuses for behavior. It means we understand that any human, no matter how hardened, simply craves love. Somewhere, someway, their concept of love got warped. They were never shown what pure love looks like. Some gross perversion found its way into their life, and so they became a person who is easy to hate.

Love means we still know they can be forgiven if they repent. They're still worthy of asking for and receiving forgiveness if their heart means it. Yes, we must hold criminals accountable. Yes, they will serve their earthly punishment. But don't you want that person's heart to change from evil? When we demonize someone, we create an excuse for them to keep that hardened heart. We're saying we don't want them to change; we just want them to be miserable. Instead, we should encourage their evil to desist. If you want more love and less hurt in the world, offer more grace.

I offer these celebrity and serial criminal examples because humility is no small matter. If you care only for the poor, for friends, and for family, you are not humble. If we don't care about hard-to-love people, our hearts are as cold as theirs. When you talk about the richest of the rich and about the lowest of the low, listen to yourself. Don't say anything behind closed doors you wouldn't say with that person in the room. Cliché? Yes. True? Definitely. If you would say something hurtful with that person listening, your heart is not in a good place.

"I'm just sassy. All the ladies in my family have a fiery attitude. I say it how it is." No, nope, hell no. This is insecurity. Ask yourself why you deflect with attitude. What walls are you putting up? Being humble is being vulnerable. Why is it hard to be vulnerable? Hold yourself accountable—answer the question.

CHAPTER 8

GENDER DIFFERENCES IN HUMILITY (AND WHY THEY MATTER)

I first noticed the differences between the two genders' pride and humility about three years ago when I was reading this amazing book called *Captivating* by John and Stasi Eldredge. The book talks about the splendor of women's hearts. It's not a how-to book; it explains our femininity in a way that has never been laid out before. It brought so much healing and insight into what my heart truly desires as a woman. I sobbed while reading this book every night.

I felt all the things the book described. As I read, I learned of differences so vast that I don't think most men are capable of understanding humility in the same way I do. I learned to be extra-forgiving to my husband, who did not seem to understand why it was so important to compliment me on all the plants I put in our home. Living in a beautiful decorated house is last on his list of things his heart cares about. I still ask him from time to time if he likes all the new furniture and decorations I've added. He always kind of nods and says, "Yeah, looks good," just to get me to stop asking. Knowing the way his home was "decorated" before we were married, I don't know if I can even take his opinion on decor seriously. He is the kind of guy who would just have a couch and a TV. That's all he needs.

Reading *Captivating* made me realize I don't need to strive to be a "masculine" version of me to be strong and successful. That embracing my feminine nature is what makes me strong and capable of doing things a man is not fully capable of. That said, I have been seeing something remarkable in the world around me. You've probably noticed, too, that there are more female leaders now than ever. I truly believe we as females have been able to rise up and lead in ways we have never been able to before because of our ingrained mental ability for humility. I truly believe that, biologically, our brains can handle humility in a way that is harder for males. We have spent thousands of years serving men to better themselves, never letting ourselves surpass, only living to place the needs of others before our own. Thousands of years of practiced humility.

We now live in a day and age that finally recognizes us for what we are: powerful, graceful, merciful, loving, and dedicated. People today have such a need for genuine connection and raw emotion, and the old way of handling things is so empty of empathy and love. People are sick of robotic ways of business and leadership, with the boss on the top and his workers underneath him. We have shown that leadership can also include a merciful, safe, and nurturing environment. People are realizing the lack of love and nurture in the workplace, and women have especially stood up to put a stop to this cycle.

I believe male and female brains were built to handle different things, and we equally complement each other's faults. But I have seen time and time again that the foundations for the workplace mostly built by men were built in order to be functional (men are great at making things functional) but not necessarily nurturing. Workplaces have always been so stressful and morale such a challenge, and just now people are starting to practice real empathy in the workplace because women have prioritized it.

I am so grateful for the women who have shown up to make the world a better place. Raising children, working full-time jobs in order to provide and nurture. Never for themselves but always for others. They stride in patience and understanding, watering all the people around them.

A humble woman basks in the glory of others while also gleefully taking any praise she receives. One of men's biggest downfalls is their ability to be passive and just let things happen without confronting them. That is a form of pride; it's selfish and it's hurting the world around us. It is so important for men to be humble enough to be okay with confronting and facing the truth. It's okay to be softhearted and to stand up for those who are weak and need your support.

Men need to be holding other men accountable, because the way things are going will slowly break down all the safe walls men have created to be able to get away with monstrosities. It's coming to light, and the BS is getting uncovered by women who are sick of the BS and taking matters into their own hands. We are sick of the lack of fathers to our kids; we are sick of the lack of empathy; we are sick of being undermined and not taken seriously; we are sick of being an afterthought.

Now, this is not a whole chapter dedicated to shitting on men. Females, I also have some words for us—I just wanted to bring light to the fact that I recognize how we have stepped up and brought beauty to dark places. It was something we so desperately needed. It's hard in a world that is mostly male dominated.

Now, to get real to all the females and also hold you accountable, here we go.

This is not a fast pass to be able to push men down and try to rise above and over them. It is still crucial to be humble, and being humble is realizing that we are no better than anyone else. Yes, own your strengths, be confident and walk in your power, but do not think that makes you superior to anyone. We all still have blood in our veins; we are all just human. Learn to step down and let someone else do what you are not best at. You do not need to fix the world alone; you do not need to stay single because you are a strong, independent woman who doesn't need a man. No! The world still needs men and their masculine energy. It complements us in so many ways, and we have to still be thankful to males for all the good they have brought us. Our journey is not to push them away and topple them off the top; it's to join them at the top and learn to stride together. Learn to teach each other what we know and water each other's gardens. Your mission is also to raise up men, not just women. We need to watch the way we talk about men. Thousands of years of oppression does not make it okay to be condescending to men. Being condescending is not okay, ever, to anyone. That is not the kind of world we need to create.

I don't like being treated like a victim. I don't believe I'm a victim. I live in a world where good and bad things alike will happen to me, and I realize that and understand there will be times I will be treated unfairly, and that's life. I believe acting like a victim or being a product of my faults is a form of self-pity and self-focus. It's always putting my problems before others. It's sitting in my dark hole and saying the world hurt me and I'm not responsible. You are responsible for your inner peace—there is no blaming. If you are bitter, hurt, have mental illness, or are even physically sick, you are not a victim. Well, unless you choose to be. If you continue to reiterate all your problems and just let them continue to be problems instead of lessons to help you grow, then you are just feeling bad for yourself, which is selfish because it's being self-focused. A "woe is me" attitude is not okay and should not be a lifelong anthem.

Yes, there are times of mourning in our life. If we lost a job, lost a loved one, got diagnosed with something terrible, or had something terrible happen to us. It's okay to mourn for a time when we are hurt, but it is not okay to sit in it as a victim. We are as free and happy as we allow ourselves to be. I could go into all the inspirational stories of people who have nothing but somehow have found happiness in the worst of situations. We all know those stories, and we all know by now that happiness is a state of mind. It's not dependent on money, success, friendships, family members, world events, politics, losses, or hurt.

Take responsibility for your happiness. Don't sit in your sadness. Get help if you need help. Exhaust every effort to get better. I have been diagnosed with four mental illnesses.. I don't choose to sit in it. Although for many years I did, and I learned many lessons from those pains. I'm the happiest I have ever been in my whole life because, after years of work, tears, and wanting to give up the fight, I finally freed my mind despite circumstances I couldn't control. That is why we must overcome it, because if we are so hell-bent on controlling things, we will always lose. We must first be okay with where we are, and then change comes. I'm not saying a depressed person should magically choose to be happy, but we must choose at some point to exhaust every effort to find what will work. If you talk about how depressed you are every day, chances are you will continue to be depressed every day. If you talk about being overwhelmed every day, chances are you will stay overwhelmed.

We have to watch our words and thoughts. With small and steady changes, you can change your mind. You attract what you put out. Take responsibility for your thoughts and actions. I don't mean this to be harsh. I have dealt with clinical depression and anxiety for years. It wasn't until I had my second son, after years of rejecting the idea of seeking medical intervention, that I decided to get professional help. A few years later, I decided to listen to audiobooks, and that's when my life went from 50 percent to 100 percent. It completely shifted my mind and how I controlled my thoughts. I believe we all are capable of the same power I found within myself to transform our minds, and that is why I'm saying all of this.

Also, ladies, here's another thing we really need to buckle down on, and that is bitterness and unforgiveness. I remember all my grudges, from when my kindergarten teacher told me "Sit your little fanny down!" to when my elementary school teacher called me a rude child in front of the whole class. I know most females can relate. We can remember incidents portraying our inability to forgive people so well that we could literally reiterate word for word what Rachel said to piss us off in kindergarten—the audacity of that lollipop-stealing rude-ass!

But seriously. We have a true bitterness problem. I know you can think of a few people who hurt you that you feel bitterness toward. We need to deal with it. As someone who was bullied and broken by peers to the point I dropped out of high school, take it from me: we need to deal with this hurt and forgive, even if we did nothing to deserve it. This is part of taking responsibility for our hearts. We are the only ones who can keep our hearts in check.

This also applies to how we talk about other females. I can't tell you how many times I have seen a beautiful woman walk into a room, and then I hear another woman criticize her and put her down. Don't be someone who only has bad things to say about people. When you are with a friend, don't gossip. It's not okay; it will propagate weeds in your heart and turn you into a bitter and sorry person. You are not above another person. If you do that to someone, it just means you are insecure and need to push down on others to feel better about yourself. It sounds like obvious advice, but if it's so obvious, then why do so many women still do it? I don't care if you think Sarah is fake and materialistic because she got a boob job and dyed her hair blonde and walks with her nose in the air. If you are so worried about what someone else is doing that you need to cut them down, then you are not taking control of your happiness like you should be. Stop the comparison game. You have an amazing set of talents that are different from anyone else's. *Own them.*

Maybe the person you always cut down has hurt you over and over. Still, you are the source of your own happiness. Forgive them. You need to forgive all the hurt in order to be in control of your happiness. It's prideful to hold on to your hurt.

Another thing I see a lot from women is passive-aggressiveness. Oh boy, the stories I have, the cold and passive rudeness I have felt from women—it's incredible. Also, I have done this, a ton. I think everyone I know has.

We can't be truly forgiving while continuing to be passive-aggressive. I see it so much in the workplace. When I worked in a hospital, I would get tons of little hits and kicks from the older ladies I worked with. Always criticizing me, always trying to make me feel dumb or annoying. Always making remarks to hit my ego. And yes, I let it kill me. It ate me up inside. I was always going home so mad. That's why, when I got the chance, I was out. Escape misery at all costs, but most importantly, forgive. If people are treating you miserably, it's because they were once victims of misery, and they still are living in a victim mentality. Be a light in these dark places. Stand up for yourself, but also water their gardens. You never know what good can come from forgiving and still choosing to be kind to these people.

I would love to speak more on men and how to obtain humility, but it's kind of hard considering I am not a man and I am still frazzled as to how their brains work. Sometimes men can have an arrogant and know-it-all attitude when they are in an unhealthy headspace. But what do men do right that we women can appreciate? Here are some things I learned from my husband that really demonstrate how a man's heart shows humility . . .

My husband is godsent. He continually serves our family and never asks for a speck in return. He brings me coffee almost every day and never, ever complains or even expects a thank-you. I do thank him, unless I am being a brat that day. I know my husband is humble because his identity is his family. He is a father and a husband, and everything he does is to be a father and a husband. He shows by example that he lives to serve us. He is so humble, in fact, that I am not sure he really wants anything of monetary value. Buying him gifts is so hard when he never even knows what he wants. He is really focused on being a righteous and honorable man. So much so that it comes naturally. He is not perfect, of course, but I have observed that men truly shine in the realm of humility when they are serving others with whatever strength or power God gave them. They truly hold the power to build or destroy. It is amazing to me how much good a good man is capable of and how much bad a bad man is capable of.

CHAPTER 9

SELF-AWARENESS EXPLAINED

It is crucial for your walk with humility to be self-aware. Always being thoughtful of your words, thoughts, and actions. Always dissecting them and picking them apart. Part of self-awareness is always asking why. Why do I react this way? Why do I feel this way? Why do I still keep doing the things that don't bring me joy?

Almost every time I used to talk to my mom and sister, I was condescending. It took me so long to realize it and even more time to fight the habit I had spent years building. I didn't even know it was going on; it was all happening subconsciously. The condescending remarks were on autopilot. A lot of times, they emerged as unsolicited advice. When my mother opened up about working a lot and feeling under stress, instead of empathizing, I said, "Why do you still work there? You could have a way better job somewhere else." Disregarding her problems was not helpful or uplifting.

With my sister, I was not encouraging. I often scolded and mocked her without realizing what I was doing. I played it off as a joke, but sometimes I went too far and sounded like a stuck-up, know-it-all bitch.

Why did I respond this way toward them? Why was I also condescending to women in general? I realized I had very little empathy for women. Growing up, I had a rocky teenage relationship with my mother, and I felt rejected over and over by my female peers. I don't know exactly what happened, but at some point, how I managed relationships with other females became toxic. I wasn't a good friend and treated women like they were disposable. I realized I needed to be more aware of the way I reacted to them and needed to learn to empathize better.

This was huge for me. A big step in my humility journey. I was holding on to so much pride, thinking it was them and not me. Thinking I was right to "call them out" or believe they were ignorant compared to me. I finally started to apologize when I realized I was in the wrong. It's still a process in the making. I think this is something I will always have to be aware of in order to overcome it. It's hard to stop yourself in the middle of acting like an asshole and say sorry. No bone in your body wants to come to terms with the fact that you were wrong and then face it and apologize. Feeling vulnerable to women is so hard for me. Sometimes I want to say sorry, but I can't bring myself to do it because feeling that vulnerable makes me want to throw up. Sometimes I would rather just lie in my casket now than have to admit when I'm an asshole. I'm sure many of you can relate to that.

This is just a tiny example of self-awareness. You truly have to be actively aware of your heart and its intentions to start this journey. Even if it is something as small as tuning out when a friend is opening up, it's not okay. If you get consistently flustered when speaking to someone or you feel a pit in your stomach, ask yourself why. Do you need to step back from talking to this person? Are you projecting onto them and need to apologize? Are you expressing bitterness that you feel toward them and need to forgive them?

If certain conversations cause problems within a relationship you have, stop having those conversations and deal with whatever is hurting your heart. If you truly want to fix a relationship you are in with a family member, friend, or spouse, go to therapy with that person. Get help. Don't let these emotions fester until the blob of resentment has grown out of control.

Self-awareness is also being able to thoughtfully use your words instead of spurting them out. Will it do any good to throw my opinion in the bowl? Will it just add to the tension? Will it really fix anything to be vocal about this at this moment? Opinions are weak when they are just being spurted out constantly. I don't think I have actually seen a time when someone spurting their opinion out did any good. I realize people want to be heard and want to stand up for what they think is right. But your subjective opinion is just going to butt heads with someone else's subjective opinion. Unless you are being asked for your opinion or are in a place of authority where it matters, then opinions are unsolicited advice.

One of the best things I did for my mental health was taking my head out of the icky bucket of political arguments online. I was engulfed in everything current and political, reading everyone's posts and always putting my two cents in. You know what it did for me? Made my life small and absolute shit. I was literally spewing trash at other people who were also spewing trash. It made me unhappy, but I kept doing it because I thought being vocal about it was the right thing to do. I was so very wrong. I was causing so much harm, and, later, I realized it was all pride. I was acting prideful by giving my unsolicited opinions and caring so much about what I had to say that I very rarely listened. And besides, my political affiliation does not define who I am as a person or have anything to do with my personality. And don't get me started with how often I defended the Kardashians. I truly am a force, but I need to learn to focus my passion in a more meaningful and impactful way.

I say this because it's a *big* issue and even a bigger waste of time. I stopped following anyone who posted opinionated political stuff and totally cut out all the noise, and *wow*! I actually stopped thinking about it, I stopped paying attention, and I realized I was no longer bitter and aggravated. I was actually more compassionate. I became happy and channeled all that energy into my business and creating what I loved. I never realized how much time I wasted in that realm. It was such a waste of time and such an outlet for pride.

I know everyone doesn't have this issue or even go on social media, but I bring it up because many do. We need to be self-aware and hold ourselves accountable, and even if our opinions might be right, it's not right to cause more chaos in an already chaotic world. Let's stop hurting people and pushing the other side away. We are all just human, and I believe that every human is trying their best to be a good person. Nobody is purposely trying to be bad, unless they are a criminal or psychopath, but those people are few and far between, my friend. If you want more love in the world, be a listener, be empathetic, be self-aware enough to know that something you are doing is not serving you and not serving the people around you. We are so self-focused that we think our opinion really matters all the time. Who are we? Just human and flawed, that's all. Just a big bag of bones, blood, and skin. I hate this term when applied to humans, but we are quite literally *animals*.

CHAPTER 10

OPENING UP TO CHANGE

There were certain times I knew I wasn't ready for change. I would briefly think I was ready, but come to find out, I was just momentarily hyped up but didn't really have the willpower to allow that new venture into my life.

I think we all know what that inspired, hyped-up feeling feels like. Usually lasts a week or two. Where you get excited to start a project, you have all this energy and motivation. Then, all of a sudden, you see life for what it is, you realize you don't have time, or you hit a roadblock in your new venture and realize it's just too much. You get uninterested, discouraged, and bored. The project is no longer important, and you go back to working on the things that come more naturally.

This has happened to me more times than I can count. Being a creative entrepreneur at heart, it took me years to realize what projects I was capable of bringing into my life and what projects and business ventures were better left on the shelf.

Realizing this actually made me feel such relief. It was a stressor of mine. Always starting something new and never finishing it. Before I started a big-girl business, I was *always* doing this. Honestly, it was super discouraging. I thought I would be left in the emptiness of never-finished projects. Never good enough, never motivated enough to finish anything. It really bummed me out and made me believe I was just a lazy, unmotivated, not-good-at-anything half-assed human. How could all these other friends of mine stick to going to school for four years, get a degree, and work the same job for more than a year? Yet I couldn't even finish a painting, my laundry, or decorating my home. Any business venture I wanted to dive into soon fizzled out quickly when I realized it took work and getting people to pay me was hard.

This was also due to my having absolutely no idea what resources were helpful, who to ask, or how to start a business. I was clueless. I was a stay-at-home mom who wasn't even motivated to keep my house in order or finally create a system for my family's organizational well-being. I would get excited to meal prep, prep a whole week's worth of meals, and then *blah*, never again. A one-hit wonder. I hated repetition. I lived in fear of doing the same things every day because to me, doing the same things every day equaled unhappiness. Seeing my parents with a routine looked overwhelming. Doing the same thing every day reminded me of school, which was excruciating for me, to the point of dropping out of high school because I felt sick to my stomach returning every day to a place I hated. Routine reminded me of being stuck, being unhappy. I thought it was just something every adult had to succumb to and that somehow, I was broken and didn't know how to deal with it like the rest. I really thought something was wrong with me. I thought I was not capable of a normal adult life. I was really unbearably sad and felt there was no point to my existence even though I had a deep desire for something more, something big.

I loved my kids and my husband, but my heart just knew that wasn't all there was to life. I was restless; I was kind of freaking out, honestly. I went through a huge mental and physical breakdown. My body felt the pain my heart felt. I couldn't get out of bed. I could hardly eat through tears every day. I had separation anxiety every time my husband left for work. I felt alone, useless. I tried to tell my family how sad I was, but nobody understood.

I later realized I had been living with this burning desire my whole life, and the sadder I got, the more it burned. I was meant to go through this deep sadness. I was meant to feel the pain in order to initiate the desire I so badly needed. The pain created a huge culture of gratitude in my life for everything good that came to me. I knew what life was like without desire, creativity, and gratitude. When I came out of the pain, I rejoiced every moment. Even the smallest wins were huge. Any glimpse of joy was overwhelming to me because I had felt sadness for so many years. Even writing this now, I feel so much gratitude that I'm far away from that place.

I finally discovered how to open my heart to new business ventures and projects when I picked up my very first camera. This one came more naturally. It hit me like a ton of bricks. My destiny was finally in my hands. I lived my whole life without knowing that *this* was what I was missing.

I felt electricity when I picked up that starter camera. I knew in my heart that this was it. It's what I had been waiting for. God was waiting for me to hit my lowest so I could fully appreciate it. I was *so* grateful. Beyond measure. Words can't even explain the gratitude I felt and still feel that I found anything at all that I love to do. And could do every day without getting bored. I allowed my identity to become one with this. It became a part of my life in every way. It was a part of who I was. It was always there.

Through the journey of my photo business, I was faced with the prospect of other business ventures. A lot of them had to do with other outlets that involved photos, or thrifting and fashion-type businesses. A fun pastime of mine is thrifting; it's so therapeutic to find treasures that are completely unique. I thought since I loved it so much, selling pieces I found would make a wonderful business. There were tons of reselling apps for people who thrifted that I could make a killing on. I also could use my photo skills to take fashionable photos with the pieces I found. A win-win! Doing two things I loved at once, or so I thought.

I went out and bought tons of thrifted clothing. Gorgeous pieces that, to this day, I still treasure. I took photos of them, posted a few, but then started to realize I was too busy to keep doing it. I got super bored and didn't even list all the items I bought, and it fizzled out after about ten days.

Why? I thought. *Why am I getting bored?* I realized this type of work just did not fit with my identity. It was meant to be an enjoyable hobby for me, not a business. Some things we do that *could* make money should not make money; they should remain hobbies and creative outlets that exert no pressure to be monetized.

I had to learn this with so many things. I tried to create other e-commerce businesses that just didn't fit right. I tried to create other service businesses that just did not fill me up. I even tried writing books for all the wrong reasons, getting bored after about twenty-five pages. They weren't meant to be a part of my identity. Honestly, I was also not ready to receive these ventures as a part of my identity. It took many failed adventures to be able to discern when something was right for me or not. Now I have the insight to know when something is not for me. Sometimes. As an artist, starting projects that we never finish is just kind of our thing, honestly.

So with all that being said, I'm going to dive into how I mentally prepared to open my identity to a new business venture and allowed it to fit in with my already busy lifestyle. That was the biggest issue for me. *Time.* I could not for the life of me tackle another business if I felt the work was robbing me of my precious time.

I decided being a photographer would always leave me in the service-based industry. Wedding photography is a physical service, and as long as I did it, I was always going to be away from home, physically serving my clients. Which I love to do, but I love being home with my kids and husband also. I wish I could bring them to work with me because I miss them so much when I am gone. As extroverted as I am, I don't like being away from my home base for very long. I knew that the busier I got with weddings, the more I'd be away from home.

I decided I needed to have a separate stream of income that would allow me to do fewer weddings so I would not have to rely on photography as my only income generator.

E-commerce piqued my interest. I love being at home behind my computer working. I love the idea of building a brand and creating content for that brand. Okay, so I had this idea. But when I tried to do it on my own—launching an e-commerce store with minimal investment and minimal time put in—crickets. It was harder than I thought. Also, I had no idea what I was getting myself into, and the free course that taught me how to do it did not give me the gritty information I needed. So even though I knew I wanted to do the idea, I got busy again and set it aside. I let the discouragement sit for about six months and kept the idea in my pocket.

Luckily, a wedding photography educator, who helped me scale my photo business, also happened to be a master at e-commerce. He had multiple online stores already that were up and running and successful. I knew he could help me learn how to launch my own business. For a while, I thought of asking him personally. But one day, he announced he would be teaching an e-commerce course, and I knew I needed to sign up. I needed this in order to start an e-commerce store. I needed the accountability of having a teacher and other attendees keeping me on task. I knew I would not be able to go through the e-commerce adventure without it, but I knew opening an e-commerce store is what needed to be done. I knew what I needed to succeed.

Before I dove into this business venture, I was real with myself about what it would take and how it would feel. I knew there would be days I would be bored, discouraged, and feel like I was wasting my valuable time and money. I knew some of it would make me sick to my stomach. I knew I would cry. I knew part of me would fight it and feel like it was too hard. I was ready for all of this. I knew it would come. I knew I had to get over it mentally before it started because I decided that this *needed* to be done in order to bring in the additional income I needed to spend more time with my family. I knew I was going to be investing precious dollars without seeing the return right away.

I decided to let this business slowly become a part of my identity. I was prepared for the bad feelings that come with starting a big business venture. I was *so* excited, but over and over, I spent countless nights working on building a website, stressing about the box design, and trying to source a manufacturer and a warehouse to ship my product. It was messy. I decided with each big move, I would only give myself a few days to make a decision. I had to become very decisive. The longer I dwelled on a big decision, the more time it gave my brain to overthink and make a choice out of fear that I would lose my money or time.

I also made a few life changes during this phase of my life. I decided to go sober, and I am still sober as I write this. I knew drinking was a distraction I needed out of my life. I'm not sure I could have launched my company if I were drinking. I also listened to a ton of audiobooks and podcasts, anything I needed to pick me up or teach me something new. When it comes to my passions, my brain is a sponge for education. I could listen to business pep talks all day. I am never sitting with one idea. I'm always evolving with new information and new trends. Everything moves so fast now that you need to learn as often as you can because your industry can change in a day. That is a huge part of humility: being able to evolve, even when it is uncomfortable. Change does not feel good, and I knew that this business adventure would not always feel good, that it would push me way out of my comfort zone. Sometimes I was sick to my stomach because I was putting so much work in and had no idea if it would even be profitable. I was so scared of wasting my time. Which motivated me to do the business right, because I would not allow this to waste my time.

Being decisive, I chose to sell nail polish. I saw a gap in the industry—not very many innovative brands, and just a few really big brands that basically ruled the roost. I also looked into the market, and there was a huge estimation of growth within the next five years. I knew it was time to jump in. It felt right in my heart; it made sense. Bess & Color was born.

The key was being decisive. From the name of the company to the manufacturer that offered everything I needed. The manufacturer I chose was way over my budget. But it offered some things I believed in, and honestly, I had not found a better choice. I decided to not think too hard and just do. Failing was not an option. I mean, it was possible, but this was part of my identity now, and I was ready to make it work. This needed to work if I wanted to live the life I dreamed of.

That is the challenge for people. Just making the decision. Just getting the product you need to start, listing it on your website, and launching. Pay more if you need to and if you believe in what you're doing. But most of all, just do it. Every time fear crept in, I said, "Get out of here, scarcity mindset!" I grabbed this by the wheel and raced. I was in charge. And if it were going to fail, it would not be because of my product. It would be because of my effort. I knew I held the key to my own success. I knew there were so many others out there with products that were more toxic, not cute, and way more expensive. I mean, some dude is out there selling regular-ass potatoes with messages written on them for way too much money. If he was making a killing, so could I—but with better products.

I had to wrap my head around this project before I could do it. I had to decide *before* I was discouraged that discouragement would be part of this story. I jumped into this venture differently than I had other business adventures. I was not fueled by emotion and the idea of a new shiny business that would thrive. I was fueled with reasonable expectations that would require work. I was envisioning a practical idea that would help me have the freedom I so desired. I was chasing not the business and the dollar bills but the lifestyle of peace and quality that I wanted for my family. It was for them, not for me. That is why it made all the difference. How can you mentally prepare for a project in order to see it through?

1. For starters, be practical and reasonable! Map out all the things the project will truly take. Even make a list of how much time each step will take so you have a reasonable idea of the extent of work before you. This is true whether the project is to finish a painting or open an online store. If you lay out reasonable expectations first, you will get a better idea of what the process will be. Don't get infatuated with the end result. You must also desire the process.

2. Another thing to keep you motivated during a project is reading books and listening to motivational podcasts. Ones that especially have to do with what you are working on and what phase you are in within your project. Honestly, you need this. Even if you are motivated, this will do wonders for you. Your mind needs to be molded into this new part of your identity. You need to always hear about it, learn about it. You are essentially growing a new portion of your life, and you need to hear about it all the time until it sticks with you permanently.

3. Accountability. Often, we *do not* keep ourselves accountable. It really helps to have a group to help you stay accountable. Whether

it's a meeting you have every week with some friends to work on your projects, a mastermind video chat every week with other growing business owners, a coach to help you see it through, or a mentor. There are countless ways to find communities that will keep you accountable. Mine was joining a workshop and having that private group to always encourage me. We were part of each other's lives while we took the journey of launching e-commerce websites. Find your people! They are there.

4. Make firm decisions, and do them right away. The more you think about all the bad things that can happen, the more excuses you will make for yourself not to act. I'm not saying risk something that could destroy your whole life. Be reasonable. But also, don't live in fear. The only reason I was able to start any of my companies is because I do not fear risk. Well, I take that back. I do fear risk, but I get over it and do the thing that scares me anyway. The only difference between you and the person who is running a profitable business is they stepped over their fear and crushed it between their toes and ate it for breakfast. Most people won't take the first few steps because they are scared. That is what sets entrepreneurs and regular folk apart.

Make some big decisions and act on them. I told myself I needed to buy product ASAP for my nail polish business. I ordered as fast as I could so that I didn't have enough time to put it off and scare myself out of it. Then, after the first big step, make the next big step. And so on and so on.

How does all this tie in with humility, you might be wondering? Self-awareness is the key factor in this. Knowing your limits and understanding yourself on a deep level are critical. Having the insight to know that most good things are not made out of gold is also crucial. Good things are made out of hard work. They are labors of love, real love. Love that is there for all the right reasons and not shallow, selfish desires to grow yourself and only yourself. A business opportunity is not a pot of gold; it's an opportunity to grow joy and provide for those you love. It feeds you, nurtures you, and you become so grateful for these opportunities to exist in your life. Our desires sometimes just fizzle out because our heart is in the wrong place and our motives are all about what we can get out of them rather than enjoying the craft and creation of something that will feed and nurture us.

This is why so many business books ask you about "your why." Why do you want to have more income? It's so important to really know why and to really be able to discern if you are being true to yourself about your motives.

It's okay to realize your motives are selfish. That is great; that is a huge step to your road in humility. With every selfish motive there is a deeper motive, something more pure and real that is masked by a selfish tone. There is something deep inside that you want to bring to the world that will be beneficial and will spread the real message your heart desires to share.

CHAPTER 11

WHAT'S WRONG WITH SELF-LOVE?

The phrase "love yourself" makes me cringe. It seems prevalent in artist and entrepreneur circles, especially in the online photography business community. Basically, anyone who is reading mass amounts of personal improvement books is who would regurgitate "self-love." I truly was wondering how so many people did not see through the phrase and cringe at its sound like I did.

In 2018, I attended a business workshop. One of the guest speakers, bless his heart, spoke about self-love. I remember consciously trying to open myself up to learning about it, maybe consider it an actual thing. But as it went on, it sounded more and more empty to me. I just could not allow it to be a part of who I was. It seemed like a flimsy ideal. An ideal that would not serve me and didn't seem to be serving other people, from what I could tell. It seemed like a buzzword that took the place of "I'm working on myself." I wondered if the speaker even really believed at all that self-love helped him reach success. I looked around to see if others seemed to be into what he was saying. The crowd wasn't embracing it at all. No head nods or smiles. Just blank faces. The blank faces showed me that self-love talk is really just empty talk when you don't know how else to explain what you mean. It is a phrase people use when they have not really sat down and contemplated their own code to life. It's just a code they adopted. It sounds nice enough, right?

This is a big topic and probably a controversial one. My view on the self-love movement might go against everything you believe about it. Self-love may be the core of your moral soundness. I'm here to tell you about the holes I see in it. The very idea and definition of it is open to interpretation. If you scour the internet about its meaning, you are left with all sorts of definitions. All of which are, again, subjective and not very relatable to everyone under the sun. This is the first reason why I am not all about the "self-love" term. I feel it is too broad, open to interpretation, and not very good at conveying what people actually mean. It's not specific at all. It could mean anything from luxuriating in bubble baths and meditating to only giving a hoot about yourself and saying no thanks to anything you don't feel like doing. It's just not an accurate way of describing what we are really trying to accomplish, which is having wholeness, high self-worth, and joy within ourselves. We desire contentment and inner peace. We want to bloom into who we are meant to be and not feel suppressed and unworthy because of who we are.

The self-love movement has led a lot of people to think that being self-focused, or selfish, is okay. The self-love movement often masks selfishness as loving oneself. Not always, but as I said, the definition is open to interpretation, and people who are not emotionally mature don't understand what true self-love looks like. Also, sad to say, most people are not very emotionally mature. I know so many intelligent people who embrace the buzzword of self-love because, well, first of all, it sounds nice and shiny. Sounds right and promising. But those people can probably not really articulate what in their hearts they *really* mean when they say they want to love themselves. As I said, what people really want is wholeness.

A lot about self-love is putting yourself first, cutting out "toxic" people from your life, and avoiding things you don't want to do because they don't "serve you." First, note that the toxic person may be you. Just because you have a rough relationship with someone does not mean you aren't to blame as well. As I said, often when we have issues with people, it's because we haven't allowed ourselves to forgive. I'm not saying don't have boundaries, but don't just reject everyone who isn't up to your standard. If you want to live a happy and whole life, you must be able to coexist with people who have hurt you. Being able to forgive and set boundaries but still maintain a loving heart toward them.

Often if you have too many toxic people in your life, you might be contributing to this recurring problem. Why is it a constant theme in your life? What about you makes you an easy target for these people? Maybe your offense threshold is too low. Humans are just human. They will never be fully reliable. Some things these people do to hurt you are not about you at all but about them and their hurt. When you meet trials within your relationships with rejection instead of forgiveness, you are doing yourself a disservice. Bitterness is piling on, and your heart will become more and more clouded as you think you are serving yourself when in fact you are imploding your own well-being. Also, don't take this as "victim blaming," another wonderful buzzword. If someone is truly awful to you, then of course you may have to remove them completely.

I also have a hard time with the concept of "self first" that the self-love movement promotes. Everyone knows when you are on a plane, you put your own oxygen mask on before helping your fellow passenger. Sometimes this is necessary in life, but I feel like we get stuck in the "put mine on first" mentality and completely forget that we are meant to put ours on first so we can help the people next to us. It is our duty to pick ourselves up from the ashes so we can serve the rest of the world and not just ourselves. People spend so much time working on things that serve them personally that they never learn how to serve others. I believe we will never be happy only serving ourselves. Real wholeness is learning to serve the rest of the world with whatever gifts we were given.

The self-love movement promotes the individual. Nothing about just myself accurately represents what I really want out of life. I see mostly women saying how they need to love themselves first before they can love someone else. Translation: "I don't feel great about who I am. I'm insecure and I feel like I'm unworthy of love and properly loving someone else correctly. I want to focus on doing what I want, because I'm not ready to serve anyone but myself."

I believe the self-love movement has made a way for people to say that they don't want to serve others. Now, again, this is all up for interpretation. Maybe self-love can be expressed in a pure, unselfish, humble way. Still, the movement has shown me why it does not truly define wholeness for people. It is super vague, and I think we could explain the concept in a much more specific way.

Living in wholeness, self-worth, and joy exemplifies how we serve and get along with other people. Life is not about "doing you, boo." I joke and say, "Yay, do you," but it's not a life motto. I don't make every decision based on doing something for myself and pretend that pushing away relationships and friendships is empowering me. Yes, these things are hard. You might not feel good right away. It might be a hard journey and feel uncomfortable, but life is all about getting out of your comfort zone. You cannot evolve into a great person without testing and challenging your ability to serve the world before yourself.

We can't live in the moment of just doing what feels good now. That is so fleeting. Life is about the long term, the long haul. Sure, it might be hard for a few years or maybe your whole life to forgive your parents. But your heart will soften, your compassion will grow, and your wholeness will emerge. Most things that are good for you are not instantaneous. Going out and partying every week while surrounding yourself with people who are living in the moment rather than seeking internal wholeness is not self-love, it's self-destruction.

To conclude, we could much better convey what we mean when we say self-love. People who have just heard it as a buzzword and have adopted it into their life mottos because they haven't found what they really stand for yet are hurting and not helping themselves.

CHAPTER 12

INTENTION I

One of the biggest challenges I faced during this journey of understanding when my pride made its debut was learning how to dissect my intentions. I feel like it's really easy for our brains to create a reasonable narrative to explain whatever it is we are desiring. We defend our ideas with words that sound right, but it's not necessarily where our hearts are or what our hearts are really after. We even seek advice from people who we know will give us the answers we want rather than objective advice from people who will make sure our hearts are in the right place.

For example, after having my second son reach an age when he was more independent, it became easier for me to have a social life again. I started going out on weekends and drinking with my friends, never inviting my husband, because I just wanted some peace and fun with my girlfriends.

My husband disapproved of me always going out and drinking every chance I got. I told him, "Don't be controlling. I'm an adult, Jeff. I know I'm not doing anything wrong when I go out, and I just want to go relax with my friends. I'm super extroverted, and I just want to be around people, listen to music, and hang out with my peeps." I saw all my friends my age still going out. Even some just like me who had kids and a spouse. If they were all doing it, and they were all contributing members of society, then what was wrong with my doing it? I wasn't doing anything wrong. I just wanted to have fun.

Thinking about these past choices actually hurts my heart. My husband was right: it wasn't appropriate. It's not like I was casually sipping drinks poolside with a couple of friends. I was partying, and partying way too hard. I had kids at home, and going out and drinking all the time was not the mature thing to do. Not only that, but I was actually making myself sick all the time with how hungover I was. I was so exhausted that it took me days to recuperate and be able to get back to work. I was slacking on everything. My home, my work, my kids, my husband, and myself.

I pretended my husband was being controlling, but he was seriously looking out for me and challenging me to be a better person. He never told me no, but I knew he disapproved. I was not respecting him and his wishes, even though he respected mine and always put things aside for me. I was walking all over him but not respecting the few wishes he wanted me to follow. I was only thinking about myself and not about him or our kids.

What was really going on in my heart was that I was stressed. I was overwhelmed. I was bored. I was honestly starting to lose purpose. I was living in the now, doing what made me happy at that very second and not working on my eternal happiness that would last a lifetime. I was building myself up with surface-level things, and it was disintegrating everything underneath. I was hurting, and I masked it with the idea that "I just needed more." I couldn't stay locked up in the house anymore. I wanted to turn off and shut off. I used alcohol as a way to reset. But the more I used it, the more I needed to reset . .

. until I reached the point where I was always shutting myself off and unavailable to everyone. Even myself. I was a wreck.

It all came crashing down when I got so drunk one night after having about ten drinks at a Vampire Weekend concert that I threw up blood. Insert vampire joke. I'm pretty sure all the drinking gave me a serious stomach ulcer, and I'm pretty bummed that I got so drunk during one of my favorite bands' concerts.

That is when I quit drinking. When I quit, it was like gold rained from the heavens. My life went to a whole new level. I was blessed with so many things that God was probably holding out on me until I got my act together. We got the news that we won a settlement with our insurance company after years of battle over losing our home and essentially getting screwed over by the big-money man. With that settlement we were able to buy a new forever home. Which was incredible considering we had moved seven times within six years with all our kids. We were sick of it. We needed a place to settle down and call home. A place we actually loved. Which is exactly what we found. I got to decorate how I wanted and buy countless houseplants to turn our home into a jungle. I started my nail polish company, my photography business was thriving, and I was getting opportunities that seemed unreal. All of a sudden, everything I desired started happening. It literally made no sense. It's like all these opportunities were waiting to burst through the door. We even hosted Thanksgiving, and I threw a huge surprise party for my husband. We also bought a kitten to accompany our older cat, which was a longtime desire for the whole family. (Note: Our older cat is less than amused with the kitten. The kitten sure does love him, though. In case you are wondering—and you probably aren't—the older cat's name is Jack and the baby is Peter, short for Peter Pan. Yes, my cats have human names.)

Basically, all my kitten and plant dreams were coming true. The holidays were magical, and the kids finally had a home big enough to contain their endless toys. Mostly, I was happy. For the first time in my life. And it was real happiness, not alcohol induced and not fleeting. I had stable, eternal, deep joy. It became clear that I had to go through the bad stuff first to better understand the good; I had to feel low. I had to get dragged in the dirt to know how good it would feel when I got to the other side. I needed to live a life of sadness to know the difference between a mediocre life and a life full of meaning.

I started to play music with my dad, which was a longtime desire of mine. I always had a passion for singing. I always knew I wanted to do it, and as often as I would try to get my dad to make music with me, it would just never work out and we could never agree. It wasn't until I got into this "service" mentality that my intentions became clear. Playing music was never something I wanted to do just because I loved it; I wanted to do it to build up my own ego. Once I didn't care about my ego anymore, playing a tambourine and singing songs with my dad happened naturally. I took my ego out of it, and I let him lead the way, his way. When I stopped trying to control the situation, what I actually wanted (the pure and humble motive) happened! It allowed me to bond with my father artist to artist. Music was something we both had in common that we could do together. It brought joy to our whole family to see us play together and shower them in song as he shredded on the guitar and I flexed my vocal cords and tapped a mean tambourine.

This is also when I started to write. See, I knew I was always a writer, deep inside me, but I got bored with everything I wrote, and it always fizzled out and never got finished. I had long dreamed of writing a book. A book about what, you might ask? Good question. I've tried everything from poetry to postapocalyptic novels to self-help-type things that were not very helpful at all.

This came naturally. One day I had a thought and jotted it down. Before I knew it, I had a ton of thoughts on this subject and kept going and going until I realized it was long enough to become a book. And I loved being able to organize my thoughts. Explaining it in fifteen minutes was just not enough time to understand what had taken me a lifetime to figure out.

I cast my ego aside. I always wanted to say I had written a book because I wanted to feel pride. I wanted to use the title "writer" so that when people asked, "So what do you do for work?" I could say, "I'm a photographer, and I write books; no big deal," as I sip my cappuccino and smoke my pipe wearing sunglasses in the dark and mysterious corner of a coffee shop in New York or Paris. I literally was so into boosting my ego that I was looking forward to bragging about being a writer more than actually being passionate about writing. I saw the end before I saw the journey in between. But right now, my friends, I am enjoying the journey of writing so much that my heart is bursting with joy. It has become a part of my identity.

I decided to only write when I felt like it and without intentions. I knew humility was something I was passionate about, and I essentially wanted to map it out in a book. Obviously, as an artist, I want to share it with people. I don't want to keep all this information locked away. In fact, I think learning about humility is crucial, and it is my calling, my job as a human, my duty, to share and spread this message. It's not about me gaining; it's about me giving to the world. It's about helping people change their hearts. It's about revival. I want people to feel the same joy I feel. I want the people around me to realize the world is at their fingertips if they can just kick their pride to the side and invite humility into their identity. My intentions made all the difference. When my intentions were wrong, I was unable to write a book. I wasn't even aware at the time that my intentions were wrong. I thought I just wasn't trying hard enough and I wasn't disciplined. I was so wrong. I was getting bored because my pride was not a good motivator for wanting to finish a book. Shocking, right? Insert laugh emoji.

Remember, I didn't even see this pride. It was hidden deep inside. Once I gave up the steering wheel and stopped trying to micromanage and control my life, the things I always desired fell into place the way they were supposed to, not the way I was trying to force them. It's not that I wasn't meant to write. It's that I was meant first to learn a lesson, stop drinking, gain real joy, and then have something to write about.

Intentions have so much to do with being self-aware. Being self-aware is hard. It's basically getting to the point where you are considering all alternatives. You are stepping outside yourself and seeing it for what it is. It's about trying to have the most unbiased opinion about your feelings as you can. You know when a friend says you hurt them and you immediately get defensive because you know you didn't mean to and their being hurt is not your fault? Being self-aware is being able to accept that maybe the alternative could be true. Maybe you did hurt them; maybe you were wrong. Does that mean you were wrong? Not always, but in all situations, all you can do is hold yourself accountable. Sometimes people accuse you because of their own pride and shortcomings. When that happens, all you can do is control your reaction. All you can do is understand that some people are not ready to look at themselves.

Please don't take that as an opportunity to tell someone to chill and be a little humbler. Take it as an opportunity to exemplify how you would hope someone would react to you when you confront them. The best way to lead is by example. Finger-pointing and blaming will just hurt feelings, even if they do it to you first. Don't stoop to their level if you truly feel like you did not wrong someone, but only after you have stepped out of yourself and faced the uncomfortable reality that you could have truly hurt them.

We should never get too comfortable with who we are and stop evolving. If every year you don't look back and see an improvement in who you have become, then something may be wrong. You may need to heal and snap out of your slumber of stagnation. It might feel safe to stay in your comfort zone. But you are holding yourself back and pushing away the opportunities that God has for you. These opportunities are just waiting to be put to good use, and all that's needed is for you to wake up from your slumber, decide everything is not as fine and dandy as it seemed, and know you have some mental and emotional work to do.

My intentions have been flawed. I used to be obsessed with wanting to go on mission trips when I was a teenager. I thought my life calling was to travel to remote countries to bring them a helping hand, teach kids, provide food, etc. I wanted to become a traveling journalist and document my mission trips. Harmless enough, right? I mean my dream was to basically save the world and spread love— how could that not be the right thing to do?

Well, for starters, I had an awful relationship with my parents at the time, would try drugs recreationally, and was in my first serious relationship, and it was with a man significantly older than me. Basically, I had no business going overseas to preach about wholeness to people who needed stability rather than a teenager with a seriously crap attitude. I was convinced it was my true calling, though. Honestly, to this day, I still think it is. I just don't think it's for me yet. I was so blinded by the idea of bettering the world that I saw nothing wrong with my maturity level. Well, my friends, when I became an adult, I realized that my intentions were not for other people at all. I was a broken person, and I was looking to fill myself up with meaning by doing something actionable. Helping those in need gives people meaning, right? I had such a hard time seeing that my heart was not mended enough to help people. It took years for my heart to be in a place to truly serve others in a way that really was not about myself. In a way where I don't even need to hear a thank-you or any type of praise. Now I do it because I know I need to in order to please God. I do it not to make myself feel good but to give off the little bit of goodness that I have because I'm so grateful that I have the joy I have. I have so much that my cup is overflowing, and I want to water other people with it. When you are truly happy, you don't keep it to yourself.

I was so sad as a teenager that I was trying to run away. I was trying to find meaning in travel and escape. I romanticized being somewhere far away and journaling about all the cool things I saw. I thought my dream was *so* unique. (I am such a millennial that it hurts. Eye roll.) But I was not ready to devote my time to other people on that level yet.. Quite frankly, I had nothing to offer them. I wasn't a good role model. When I wasn't even a good friend to the people I knew, how could I be a good stranger to people who were in desperate need of real love?

I know this kind of giving is something my future holds, but maybe not in the way I thought it would. Maybe I will end up adopting, fostering, or funding orphanages. See! That's another thing. I was *not* a kid person when I was a teenager, but now I love kids to my core and would cherish helping kids in need. Either locally or remote. Or both! I do support some missionaries and give to nonprofits that help kids, but I know I will pursue this more in my future. I just know if I keep leaving my heart open for God to guide me, I will make it to whatever destination he has set out for me.

CHAPTER 13

LOVING WHEN YOU DON'T WANNA

When I talk about modern-day humility, I am not writing about ancient proverbs that talk about being humble. I'm talking about how current situations we face every day are testing our humility. It's harder than ever to be humble. It's even harder to detect. It's not as cut-and-dried as "care about others more than yourself."

Being humble in this modern age is about cutting out all the noise. It's harder to make sense of old ways of viewing humility. There are very few resources about how to apply humility in our daily lives.

"Just love yourself" feels easily adoptable, while "fill yourself with eternal joy and cast out your pride" sounds way too complicated, like too much work. People think, *I will just love myself and hope joy decides to pop its head up somewhere along the way.*

Sometimes something sounds good, but when we look closely, our heart is often focused on a desire to raise our ego up. Ego and pride can sometimes be hidden by slogans like self-love or the idea that you are just cutting out toxic people in your life.

I have made so many excuses to hide my pride and mask it with other things. I'm done with the excuses. I have come to terms with telling myself, *Yes, this desire was totally selfish and all about boosting my pride.* Like me, people may give up on relationships too soon due to pride telling them it's okay to walk away from the people we "love" when they aren't serving us how we think we deserve. If you are treating a relationship that way, then perhaps you have been too focused on getting your needs met to really care about the deep needs of the other person. Love is not about only loving people that love you the way you deem necessary. Love is not about giving up on relationships when our imperfect expectations are not met. Love is not about giving up on someone who is causing you problems because it's getting too hard for you. You are not loving deeply enough if you are breaking under such small trials. Loving other people is not about what you get out of it. Love does not have ultimatums. Love does not have expectations of how it will be loved in return. Love just loves. Even when it's hurt, it still loves, it still understands, it still forgives. Love asks itself, "How do I react to this hardship in love?" It asks, "How do I love those who don't love me?"

If we are not acting out of love, we are acting out of pride. Real love is always humble. Real love is deciding to love even when you aren't loved back correctly.

This love talk is not all about romantic relationships; it's also about friendships and family relationships. Is it okay to have boundaries? Absolutely.

The divorce rate is *so* high because people have been told and conditioned to think that love is conditional. That when it gets hard, it's okay to "do you" and get that "toxic person" out of your life and say peace out. I would go as far to say that if you are that impressionable and if you think that way at all, then maybe it's not a good idea to get married. At some point in almost every relationship, it gets agonizingly hard, you aren't doing what you want anymore, and you will make up excuses as to why this human has become toxic to you. Whatever the hell that means.

I've been there. I've done it. I've convinced myself so many times that all my frustration was caused by my husband, that he was making my life agonizingly difficult, and we were so different that he would just never understand me and be able to love me the way I needed to be loved. Turns out that I, in fact, was the toxic and selfish human in the relationship, and I was always taking and never giving. I was not truly loving him. My love was conditional. Because he was not meeting certain needs, I decided that he was just not loving me correctly. The way I deserved. A big LOL to that. I thought I was worth more, when I didn't even realize that he was loving me far more than I was loving him. His love was unconditional; my love was conditional.

Even as I write this, I am kicking myself for being so snippy with him today. Boys and girls, I am on the struggle bus with y'all! I still have so much pride built up in me. But the fact that I know it's there and I can call it out and be more aware of it is humility in the making. Pride is sticky. It's a mess. It's everywhere. In our relationships, in the things we own and the things we say. In the modern world, it has really woven its way into our culture and has become normalized.

Here is something else I see a lot: one-upping each other. Saying, "Oh, I've been there, done that." Or, "I've moved on from what you are talking about. I'm higher than where you are right now or what you seem interested in, because I'm over that thing or that phase. Let me tell you about something cooler and dismiss something you said that you were proud of. Let me one-up you and tell a funnier, crazier story because I cannot bear to not have the most ridiculous story in the room and outdo you in every way."

It's a way to put someone under your foot. It's extremely dismissive and condescending. It happens all the time, even when we don't notice. Some of you might have felt this from someone else. I know I have. Sometimes it's not even obvious we are doing it or that we are trying to put ourselves above someone else. Sometimes we cannot bear not to be the center of attention. It's petty. Like the lowest form of petty. And guess what? I've done this *so* much.

When my heart is not right toward someone, this side of me usually comes out. One example is with my husband's ex-wife. She and my husband share a son together. So she is basically in my life to stay, as is my stepson. This was hard for me. Probably the biggest emotional mountain I ever had to surmount. I not only had to get over the fact that my husband was married to someone else before me but also that he shared his first child with someone else. It was so heartbreaking to me that I didn't think I could stay with him because I felt cheated out of being his first marriage and the mother of his first son. My heart was in the mud over this, and my claws came out so many times. I would cut her down all the time.

It took me years of inner turmoil and jealousy to finally learn to love his ex-wife. She is not a bad person at all. In fact, she has been wonderful and so patient, even during times when I was an absolute rude asshat. I am actually lucky he does not have a crazy ex and that she has been easygoing in sharing their son equally and fairly. We are so blessed that she has dealt with the situation humbly and maturely. I know in many cases, divorces can be messy. In our case, it was not, and we all learned to get along and even spend many birthday parties and attend school events together as one giant family. All our kids are close. And even though maybe God did not intend for it to be this way, he placed us all together very strategically. God knew I could handle this, even though I felt like I couldn't for a while. He knew I needed to face this head-on and learn to love someone I did not intend to love when I imagined being married as a little girl.

I spent years having nothing good to say about her, being passive-aggressive and blowing up every once in a while. Granted, I was *very* young when I got married to my husband. I was nineteen years old. I was nowhere near emotionally mature. And oh boy, by the end of all this, I'd aged about two decades within a few short years. I got hit in the face with life, had two kids of my own, and was also taking care of my stepson half of the week.

God took away all the pain I felt. I was able to forgive my husband for being married before me. I was able to forgive his ex-wife for being his first love. I was able to forgive them both for sharing a child together that was not mine. I was able to love her and her son. I was able to be thankful for them and not be able to imagine a life without them.

Is it still hard sometimes? Yes, of course. I am not sure some of the jealous feelings ever go away. Maybe they do. I think the bigger point is to love despite the emotions. I recognize that they are wrong and try not to act on them or make decisions based on them. The big part is that the inner turmoil is gone. My heart was able to move past it. I was able to see my husband's true love for me and not feel like a part of it was spent. I was able to see God's love for me. I was able to see that, without this imperfect situation, my life would never have been as radiant as it is now. I was never meant for a smooth path. A smooth sea never made a skilled sailor.

This is what modern-day humble is all about. I wanted to give this really modern example that is very common now. It's okay to feel the pain. But it's not okay to never forgive and let resentment fester and destroy you. With growth, you will overcome feeling hurt and acting out. With growth, you will become exhausted with yourself, and your eyes will open to brighter and shinier things in life. With growth, you will decide to let go and forgive.

In a modern-day world, we are affected by these modern-day problems. Most of them cause a lot of inner hurt. A marriage is not meant to break, but more and more often, they do. Causing hurt and broken homes in their wake. There are so many hurting people. If you can learn to love, and I mean truly love in this modern time where love is so fleeting, your heart will have more freedom than the majority of people have in theirs. If you have gotten a divorce and you feel like you are now baggage to someone else because your marriage broke, know that you aren't. You have a big mountain to climb, but on the other side is a flowered meadow of grace and fulfillment. Once you climb over that mountain, you are capable of such great things. You never lose; you only learn.

You see, for a while, when I was married and started having kids, I thought my life was over. I felt like I had no purpose anymore other than to be a mom. I felt this way because there was a burning desire in me that was not filled yet. A desire I didn't even know existed until I finally found the things that filled it. My life, in fact, had just started. I had no idea. I wasn't stuck at all. In fact, I was stuck *before* I had kids and got married. I would have never been the person I am today if all these things had not happened in the order they did. Just when I thought I was at my lowest is when it came raining down on me.

I had to get to a really humble point in my life where I basically thought I was only meant to lie low, be a stay-at-home mom, take care of my family, and live a very simple life. All these things by themselves did not fill me. But they needed to happen. I needed to get to a point that was very far away from who I was meant to be. I needed to feel that loneliness that I think a lot of stay-at-home moms can relate to. Once God saw I was willing to stay in that place and live a simple life, he said, "*Psych!* Here is a basket of awesomeness and the ride of a lifetime."

I give all the credit to practicing humility. I stepped out of my pride, which was very hard for a young girl who was hardly emotionally mature. Now I'm a mom, but a badass mom. A mom who gets to show my kids how to be full-time artists and teach them emotional intelligence and kindness. I get to share all the great things I learned after going through that hard time in my life, and now my kids will get amazing advice from me because of all the mountains I climbed.

CHAPTER 14

HUMBLE RICHES

I don't recommend giving up all your earthly desires to live in poverty because it is wrong to desire anything at all except doing good works for the world. Part of being able to give is to reach a point of pure joy within yourself. Your cup needs to be full and overflowing for you to be able to be emotionally available enough to be the best version of yourself. God made you with a grand purpose in mind, and that grand purpose cannot be fulfilled unless there is real joy in your life. To reach joy's potential, your life has to be in balance. You probably won't be very joyful if you can barely afford to eat or pay your bills. We need to be self-aware enough to know that we can help people more when we have more resources.

Money is not evil, but the desire for it can become evil if our desire is rooted in pride. If we are truly only building our egos, then our intentions are wrong. But if we want money so that we can be comfortable, free up our time to be with family and friends and give back to others who are in need, or write a book about humility, then those desires for wealth are not wrong.

My number one goal for working hard at my businesses to earn more income was so I could make enough money to scale back on working so much and spend time with my family. It was about having peace in my home and not always stressing about work and paying the bills. When I'm stressed, I'm emotionally unavailable to my family. Earning a comfortable income is important to our inner peace. I know my heart is in a better place when I can make more money and better balance the world and my family.

I don't daydream about fancy cars or being the coolest person in the room. I daydream about sitting in a cabin in the mountains with my kids and husband, taking photos on my film camera, and making a photo book of our vacations and precious moments.

Getting a fancy car isn't wrong, but if your desires only manifest in material things and earning a higher status, then you are on a road that will leave you heartbroken.

Being stagnant in a low place is not the same as being content. Do not limit your wealth or success because you think growing it will minimize your humility. A rich person can be humble. You can be poor and still be a prideful snob! A rich person can make the income they need to free their time so they can spend it doing their calling and fulfilling their purpose.

If you think you are a good person and have good intentions, then imagine all the good things you could do if you had extra money. It could be as simple as providing a better life for your family. Or you could donate to save the rainforest, foster pets, or adopt a child who needs a loving home. The possibilities are endless if you have more income.

That is why I take making money so seriously. Because I can do even better things if I have more of it. It's just a resource to be able to fuel a better way of living and a better way of giving back to the world. Owning a business is also such a passionate way to give back to the world. It's leaving your legacy footprint in stone. It's creating a culture,

time to pivot and redirect. Something you are doing is not working. Try again. Never stop. Never stop trying to evolve.

Saying you have really tried everything but stopped because nothing worked isn't trying. There is always a way to find happiness. Sometimes it's letting go of pride and letting it come to us a different way than we expected. Stop beating a horse to death, and for the love of cats, allow yourself to open up to what is truly trying to make its way to you. Sometimes it's not that you aren't working physically hard enough; it's that you aren't working emotionally hard enough on your intentions and ego. Read books; listen to podcasts. Fill your head with something that will help you deal with these emotions that entrepreneurs have so you can at least acknowledge them.

CHAPTER 15

WHY YOU GOT REJECTED

Across all times and places, one thing about humanity has never changed: We all fear rejection. We can all agree that we want to be loved and included by our family and peers. It never feels good to be the outsider who nobody wants to hang with. Even though most people fear rejection deeply, why do we continue to feed the monster? My honest guess is that most people have never known anything different. Some is due to emotional immaturity, and some is learned behaviors. Some of us even reject another out of fear that they may reject us first. So we try to beat them to the punch.

I understand rejection is a big deal. I suffered most of my young years in school heavily misunderstood by my peers. Made fun of and bullied for who I was. It even poured into my adult life; there were times I was bullied by adults. It made me feel shameful and naked. I felt stripped of any self-worth. I felt unloved. When I feel rejection, it's a theme that reads, "Unworthy. Ugly. Unloved. Annoying. A pest." This is why I want to teach people about rejection. I don't want people to feel the pain and shame rejection brings. It can be an overflowing and unrelenting sickness of the heart. I don't even wish it on my worst enemy because I feel everyone is worthy of feeling deep love.

The way we deal with rejection plays off how we practice our humility. How we reject others is a way to compensate for low self-esteem. Thus rejecting people in order to feel above them or because we feel too good for them is a form of pride. We are not humble enough to realize that we also do a lot of things that are equally toxic. After all, we are dealing with imperfect humans.

I'm not saying don't remove horrible people from your life. If you do decide to remove people from your life, do it sparingly, and exhaust all efforts to salvage a humble relationship with this person first before deciding your life is better without them. When you do that, you are essentially saying something is wrong with them, and you're pushing them away because of it. That is rejection. Most people have no idea they are being hurtful or hard to get along with, especially if they are fighting a battle with pride. Oftentimes in a relationship, the other person isn't always the one to blame. It's so hard to see your own faults, especially when you feel like your heart is in the right place and you're just trying to do the right thing. Humility is understanding that even though we mean well, we still could be doing it all wrong.

I was once cut out of someone's life. Totally cut off. Cold turkey. It hurt big-time. In early June 2018, I was on a vacation with my husband in NYC. We were staying in this lovely Manhattan hotel, and it was an amazing trip. We would get out of bed at midnight, walk to a bodega or diner, and get something to eat because we could. My favorite part about New York is that you can walk outside at any point in the night and find hot food somewhere close. Twenty-four-seven food is my jam.

One night, when we came back after getting food, I noticed one of my longtime friends had blocked me on social media. This wasn't simply a good friend; this was my longest running friendship. Someone I thought would always be my friend, that our differences wouldn't matter, and we could still be cool with each other.

We haven't spoken since. I would've been willing to chat in person or at least have a conversation together about what it was I could have done better. But nope. She said, "C'ya later, dude," and was okay never talking to me again.

I've slowly learned that the root of rejection is unreasonable expectations. I felt rejected because I expected my friend to fill a gap in my heart that was not hers to fill. The idea that any relationship will last a lifetime is not guaranteed. My pride was hurt because I thought that after giving my love to her, she should love me back. I thought I'd earned her love. I was sorely mistaken. She owed me nothing. My anger and hurt over her cutting me off was my pride telling me I deserved better.

No matter what, losing friends hurts. I'm not saying a loss shouldn't feel like a loss. But the expectation that you can work toward earning a friendship is not healthy. I was convinced I had tried my hardest, but after getting blocked, I realized I had not. Not even close. Maybe we could have mended things, but stuff like this happens. It will continue to happen. And I have to learn not to let my heart implode just because everyone doesn't love me and some will reject me. The truth is, we were both no good for each other, and she recognized it sooner than I did. I was so scared of being rejected that I would've held on to a toxic friendship my whole life, afraid of rejection. For so long, I couldn't bear losing any female friendship. You see, relationships with other females have always been hard for me because of my vulnerability. I was not vulnerable with many people, so the ones I did open up to, I felt like I could not lose. It took me until now, until writing this book, to see that.

Sometimes you need to take certain people out of your life. Although the other person may still feel rejected no matter how you do it, you can try to do it as gently as possible. Instead of rejecting someone,

I recommend you set boundaries, preferably without announcing them. Announcing boundaries can sound like a threat or feel like rejection. Still, set those boundaries. Like limit the time you spend together. Or mute them on social media for a time. Or decide not to share sensitive subjects with them if those subjects trigger arguments. The person may still be aware you are pulling away, but you are doing so as gently as possible. Those are healthy, humble ways to set boundaries rather than reject someone flat-out.

You're not above the other person. Just because I don't go out drinking anymore doesn't mean I'm too pure for my friends who still do. Do I surround myself with them as often? No. But they still have my love and understanding. Everyone is growing at their own pace, and to some people, drinking is a culture that is a normal part of life. I understand that people feel that way even if I don't. As humans, we tend to gravitate to people who are like us and push away those who are not. I want us to normalize sitting at a table of people from all walks of life, not just people who make us feel comfortable. Do we need to have boundaries when we are around people who are bad influences? Absolutely. But can we still learn from them or have something we could teach them? Also yes.

Staying within our bubble of comfort and rejecting others who "can't sit with us" is us sitting in our comfort zone. When we are rejecting, we are reacting out of pride. There is a big difference between setting boundaries with people, removing ourselves from their lives, and rejecting them. When we reject someone, it's meant to hurt. Even if we don't realize that's what we're doing. Sometimes rejecting someone can feel like we're setting boundaries, but we are generally making a point to make it sting a little. We really have to check our pride and be aware of the way we are setting boundaries, determining if it is out of pride or if we humbly just don't think this person is healthy for us. We then have to humbly and gently remove them.

Now, if you are in an abusive relationship, that is a much different story. Sometimes you have to rip away, almost forcefully, from certain people who are abusers, because they won't take no for an answer. I in no way want to make a blanket statement without noting there are times when gently pulling away might not be possible, but for most ordinary relationships, it is.

Where does this leave us? When you decide to understand other people's rejection of you and understand how to not reject others when setting boundaries, you will feel a sense of lightheartedness and, honestly, less drama. Rejection on both ends can cause a lot of bitterness and gossip. So when you eliminate rejection as a major source of your problems, and you replace it with grace and understanding, then a lot of the bitterness and drama you once circulated will be gone. You won't have people to gossip about anymore because you won't have an ill heart toward them. You will truly continue to love them, as flawed as they are. You will understand their hardships, and you will walk with grace and mercy. Which feels far better than being unforgiving and bitter.

CHAPTER 16

INTENTION II

I'm not an all-knowing expert. I didn't read a bunch of philosophical books before writing this or listen to a hundred podcasts about humility or personal growth. This was all learned through experience. I almost feel too uneducated to speak about it. I didn't go to college or take courses to understand any of this. I'm a plain, normal person with problems on deck. But after recognizing it, I can't stop being aware of it.

I had to decide to recognize my pride, almost had to be convinced it even existed! I had to make the conscious choice to say, "Hey, pride, I see you." And then choose humility instead. A part of that was always questioning my heart. Always asking, Is this my ego? Is this my pride? Am I doing this for the right reasons?

Well, I learned enough to write a book about it. I live it every day. Sometimes I live it pretty lousily, and sometimes I live it big. I learned that I cannot control people. It seems obvious, but the way it seeps in is not so obvious.

I spent a lot of time focusing on how the things I could not control impacted me. I would feel so much fear and anxiety over my relationships with people, over people doing things in a way I did not agree with, and finding myself in situations that fell out of my control, such as being stuck in traffic for too long and ending up late somewhere. I would even get upset seeing my friends get treated badly in their relationships when that didn't even affect me! The list goes on and on. It caused a lot of stress because I knew I could not keep these uncontrollable relationships and unpredictable situations within my safe bubble. They were open and free to jump any way they wanted, and I knew some jumping trajectories would cause a lot of stress. My expectations were too narrow. I had to strip my expectations.

Once I decided that when shit hits the fan, I will remain at peace, the raging waters stood still. I gave myself permission to let go of the things that stirred my heart in a bad way. I gave myself permission to be okay with uncomfortable situations. I was able to sleep at night knowing that all my worries were not as scary as they seemed.

I don't want to say I became carefree. But I for sure went from being particular and controlling to being able to step back and let things happen, dealing with issues calmly when they didn't go my way. I was even able to relinquish some control to other people and realize I just wasn't good at certain things; instead, I let someone else who was better at it deal with it. I was able to love people for who they were at that moment rather than always analyzing how they could change to be better. If you change for the better, great; if you don't, I will still love you. Either way, you are worthy of my love.

I talk about our expectations a lot, because they really hold us back. They really hurt us. They put us in a place where we feel very unhappy and ungrateful. Always thinking about what could be better and how we will be happy if/when _____ happens is *no* way to live. I have seen people live their lives like this. It's ungrateful, and it's negative. We have so much to enjoy now. There is so much peace for the taking. It's here for you, in this moment, if you want it.

Those big and great things won't come if your heart is in shambles and you aren't even grateful for what you have. If you are able to hear or read this, you already have a lot to be thankful for.

Of course, work for more, reach for more. I'm not saying desiring something better is wrong, but what I am saying is you still have to be thankful, and I mean truly thankful, for what you have in this moment. Every day, give thanks. When your heart is in a place of gratitude, it is open to receive more. Whether you believe in the Law of Attraction or the great Lord rewarding your gratitude with more blessings, I will say this: both are true. I can't explain it, and I don't know why it happens, but when you are focused on good things—humility, love, gratitude, etc.—other things start flowing to you. Wealth, peace, joy, opportunities galore—all start coming in. Seemingly from thin air. When you are focused on living a full life, a full life will happen. There will be no empty spaces. You will be whole, you will be happy.

It happened for me. I didn't even plan for it to happen, but it did. I wake up every day just excited to live in a house, to have a yard. To have a fridge! It is so awesome to have a well-lit home and a table that seats six. Little things, guys. Even having houseplants that are thriving just completely enthralls me. I love these little wonders and treasures that life has given me. I am so thankful to have them. Because, who am I? What made me so special to be able to live a life that I love? It was years of work on my heart.

When I first started working on my heart, I had no intention of owning a profitable business or owning a home one day or anything, for that matter. We were living in a small, overly expensive apartment with two kids and getting by on one paycheck. Barely making our bills, sometimes even being in the red. It was rough, and I felt like it wouldn't end. But I was thankful. I was not looking to build up myself in any way;

I only built up my family. I chose to serve because I believed in humility so much. I decided I would be okay staying in that place if I had to, but if I happened to move up and get an opportunity, then that was cool too!

Either way, I was thankful. I mean, it was a rough time. Now that I'm out of it, I realize I was not meant to be a stay-at-home mom forever. It was okay for that period; I needed to go through some learning and loneliness. But I decided I was going to have gratitude. And that practice of humility was somehow noticed by the heavens, and I was granted access to what was behind a long-awaited door. It was there: my whole life, waiting for me to be thankful and humble. Once I was, I realized it was me battling myself this whole time. Once I opened the door, I never looked back.

Anytime I tried to control my situation, I undoubtedly failed. I once, as some stay-at-home moms do, joined a multilevel marketing scheme to try to sell beauty products to my other mom friends, or friends in general. Well, I tried, and I failed. Horribly. I thought I was broken. *If I'm not good at this, I won't be good at anything*, I thought. Somehow, years later, here I am selling cosmetics again, successfully, when I could not for the life of me sell them years ago. Why? Intentions. Back then I was in it just to make a buck. I had these dollar signs in my eyes and this idea of running my own business. The idea itself was bigger than the effort I made. I saw myself as a successful mom doing something I didn't even know how to do. Now I am actually a successful mom who learned how to serve others and lean into the thing I was truly made for, a role I would never have discovered if I stayed a prideful and ungrateful person.

I had to go through the journey of failure. I realized that in no way, shape, or form was I built to work for someone else. I wanted to work around a culture that I created. I knew I had a lot to give, and I could not give it the way I was meant to if I was working for the standards and motto of another company. I had to make one that was a direct reflection of myself. I mean if I truly believed I had a lot of love to give as a person, I could serve clients and customers well, and a company I created would surely reflect that.

Again, intentions. My intention came from a place in which I wanted to serve others and not a place that only served me. I care so much about my customers and clients. Because of them, I am able to write all of this today. They are my team; they have helped me build my dream. You know why? Because a part of what I believe in, they believe in as well. They would not invest in me if we did not have the same intentions in mind. That is why I stay active on social media and communicate so quickly when my photography clients reach out, because I want to water them as much as they have watered me. My attention is theirs.

Our intentions can truly change our mindset. Consider a hypothetical workplace comparison: McDonald's versus Chick-fil-A. The McDonald's employee is clearly unamused, bored, and just working as a means to an end. The Chick-fil-A employee jumps at any chance to serve you and takes pride in their service efforts. Who do you think is getting off work in a better mood? I would imagine the company culture that Chick-fil-A has created has a huge impact on their employees' morale, because their job is more than just a means to an end; it's something they believe in. Not only that, but their reputation for service is unlike any other fast-food company. All because they are in the business of serving others, so much in fact that they actually created a way for their employees to comply willingly. They have given their employees some sort of desirable incentive for serving.

Now, I know *nothing* about Chick-fil-A or how they work as a company. I am just saying, it's clear that an intention to serve, and not to slave away as a means to an end, really has a huge impact. I guarantee the McDonald's employee who looks rather bored and not happy about taking my order is probably going home to complain about work. Meanwhile, the Chick-fil-A employee has run five miles through the mountains in the rain to your house because you forgot your chicken sandwich. They hand it over with a smile and a "my pleasure," then runs all the way back to work.

Geez, *intentions*. I could talk about it all day. We need to see this. We need to decide to really dissect what we are truly wanting out of something. It's like people who get into relationships too fast because they have those emoji big-heart eyes and short-term infatuation, just to find out a few months later that the heart eyes aren't there anymore. Then it happens again and again. At some point, you think these people will realize that all they are trying to do is serve themselves, and nothing will ever fill those gaps until they try to serve others. Or it's like the person who has the next new big idea . . . again . . . and all that motivation comes crashing down shortly after. Intentions. And sometimes timing. Sometimes we need to go through certain things, climb over certain mountains, before all we desire is handed to us. Once we are in a place of truly being humble and grateful for what we have, those things will come. Those big ideas will appear and work themselves out. Sometimes not in the way that we planned, but either way, we are thankful for the ride.

CHAPTER 17

TRIGGERED YET HUMBLE

There is no excuse for acting out, even when you are triggered to your core and shaken. There is no excuse, and you cannot expect forgiveness because you acted out at a low moment. We must stay consistent, constant, and reliable. We can't act out at weak moments and then get surprised when we realize we royally fucked up and the person who usually forgives us is done understanding and done with our outbursts. It's childish and immature to act that way. (I literally LOL'd as I wrote that because this is starting to read like a parenting book. Now tell your brother you're sorry and go to your room.)

Holding ourselves accountable starts in situations like this. Being a person who people can trust and rely on starts with our consistency in our reactions. Just because you had a bad day, a bad month, or a bad year doesn't mean you have earned any sort of right to an outburst. Just because you didn't get what you wanted does not give you the right to act out the chaos you might be feeling inside. There is no excuse.

You must always be in control over your emotions. Just because you see people in movies have outbursts when their life is in shambles doesn't mean we should continue to normalize this erratic behavior by indulging in it. Just because you see some sort of injustice in the world does not mean you have the right to go to extremes or outwardly react in a way that is angry or out of control. Now, there are times when acting swiftly and sternly is needed, but they are far and few between—nowhere near as often as we have normalized.

It's also not okay to constantly expect the worst in any given situation. With so many things going on in the world, it's easy to get sucked into a mentality of fear and spread that fear to others. I think this is something people don't always realize they are doing. They mask fear by saying they are being careful or prepared. You can be careful and prepared without feeling fear or inducing fear. Feeling fearful is hard. Sometimes we feel we can't control our fear. It just happens. We don't know why certain things elicit fear, but they do. My advice about fear is likely flawed because I still feel it a lot. But something that makes it possible for me to live despite this fear is hope and faith. I have an unwavering faith that I am walking in a plan that God made for me. I don't believe that plan will ever include something I can't handle, because I have total faith in God.

Now, some may say, "Gee, that's great for you, but I have suffered so much pain in my life; how is all that pain a part of any plan? I feel like it's ruined me."

It's okay to feel broken for a period. But without the hope and faith portion, it's difficult to climb away from fear. Being hopeful in any given situation is the difference between night and day. If you decide to sit in the darkness, well then, the darkness will always be there and will feel unbearable. But if you decide to sit in the light and hope for and have faith in a better future, then it will come. It always does. You decide. The battleground is in your head. Remember, there are people who have suffered more and still have gratitude. I assure you, as you read this, there are a great many people less fortunate than you who cannot read at all. And they are suffering a great deal more, yet they still wake up with gratitude. I tell you this not to minimize your pain, but to put it into perspective. Even at the lowest of your lows, there is a light at the end of the tunnel. Sometimes that light is just a peaceful heart. Sometimes that light is much greater.

The way I have handled fear and traded most of it for peace is realizing my worries are never as damned as they seem to be. I have not gotten myself into any deep shit lately. I am talking about day-to-day fears and anxieties, like business investments (money in general), wasting time, family and friend drama, etc. What I always do is walk myself through the worst scenario. When I get to the end of what the worst outcome would be, it's generally not that scary.

So that is about handling inner fear. Spreading outward fear is another hot topic. We see it often. The news and the internet are almost unavoidable. And as informative as they are, they are also redundant and feeding into fear. We can't entertain this fear. We can't become fearful from all the things we hear and then spread this fear to our peers. Because, trust me, they have seen it, they are bombarded with it, and they are probably already feeling the same dread that you feel.

Also, fear often comes out as pessimistic talk. Always waiting for a situation to turn sour or the worst outcome to happen is a very hopeless way of viewing the future. We have to stride in faith that, first of all, it's not usually as bad as you think it is and that tomorrow will be better. Be hopeful that this season will pass. Because it will.

Back when I had just quit drinking, I went with some friends to a bar because I wanted to see if going out when not drinking was as much fun. It wasn't. I was talking with a group of people I knew, and one of them asked why I wasn't drinking. I said, "Because I'm high on life. I don't need to drink." They looked at me, actually astonished, and one friend said, "Really?" My friends could not believe life could be that good. It got me thinking a lot. I actually was that happy. Unbelievably happy. For the first time in my life, it was incredible. I felt bad that so many people in that bar that night were not in a place of happiness, and they were using alcohol and drugs to mask their dread and face the music of what was really going on in their hearts.

I was there once. I was so pessimistic. I was a complainer. I'm pretty sure my complaining pushed people away. I was quite annoying in conversation, to be honest. I had nothing of value to offer the people who spoke to me because I was living in fear of my next failure. I let it manifest in my life. It was there with me every waking moment. I was allowing my fear of failure to control me. I was going to hang out at the same shady bars, surrounded by people just trying to cut out the noise, so I didn't have to face what was really going on.

But I'm telling you, once I took off the blinders, all I was hiding from was happiness. Absolute pure happiness. That is what I was pushing away without even knowing it. I thought I was fighting against more work, more things that made me unhappy, more stress, more problems. I was creating all my problems. I was scared to change because I thought this was the best life got. I was not hopeful; I didn't have the faith I have now. I was broken, and I was living in my fears so badly that I couldn't be a good friend, wife, mother, daughter, you name it! I was unstable, and I projected my fear onto anyone who got close with me. Every week there was an outburst because my stress level was so high. I had gotten to a place where I felt stuck and believed that this was all life had to offer. That was what drinking alcohol did to me. That is why I quit.

I can't stress this enough, but take every effort you can to cut out things that you use as a crutch. You will never know what your life is capable of if you are not living it soberly. I'm not saying you need to quit drinking, but if the only thing you have to look forward to is when you can drink after work, or you are living foggy from being hungover or high, then you need to wake your mind up and face the music. Medicating reality away is never going to give you the opportunity to live a life you love. If you are sad without those things, please go get professional help. I did, and I still do!

The humble reaction when we are feeling fear and turmoil is to subdue projecting our reactions to it, to react in a way that will not only calm our stress but calm the stress of others. We don't want to pretend something isn't bad if it is actually bad. But we do want to remain calm, collected, and reliable for the people around us. This might all sound very obvious. But even though it's obvious, I know you all are still acting the fool when shit hits the fan!

Also, if it's a situation that directly involves you—like let's say a family member dies—then yes, you will grieve, and that's okay. Take help from people who offer, and don't be afraid to ask for help. Also know better days are ahead. Maybe not tomorrow, but sooner than you think. If you allow yourself to find joy again, you will. And I will say it again: please get professional help if you are feeling like the pain is unbearable. Don't tread alone. Know when you've reached your limits and seek help.

It's humble to have a calm reaction because reacting in a way that is showy and over the top is just that: showy and over the top. It makes it about getting attention, or it makes it about bringing people down to your fearful level. We also cannot burden people all the time with our complaints and fears. If you find you are generally always complaining about life or drama when you are talking to friends and family, then it's time to look at yourself, because that is no way to live. Be aware of how often you complain, try to hear it, and put a stop to it. It's emotionally draining to always listen to someone complain. Your friends and family might not like your company if you are always complaining. We are responsible for the battlefields in our minds. Talking about it all the time won't fix your problem; it will just solidify and reaffirm it, bringing you deeper and deeper into the trenches.

I once upon a time thought I was being humble by complaining and putting myself down. I thought I was being humble by oversharing my worries and being overly vulnerable, thus leaving myself open to emotional attack from others. I thought making myself look lower than the people around me and making fun of myself was a humble thing. Well, it was not. It was a weak thing. I had low self-esteem, and not in a humble way. I felt unworthy, and I outwardly showed it. I left myself open to hurt many times. Bullies bullied me, even some of my friends. I would make fun of something about myself, and they would do the same. It hurt, but I shouldn't have set the example of criticizing myself, because it carved a path for other people to do the same.

Talking down about yourself or about your problems does not make you humbler. The theme of your life is not all the times you have been at your lowest. Your life theme is where you are going, not where you've been. Saying every day how hard your life is not helping you or anyone around you. It shouldn't be used as a way to make yourself look less intimidating or to gain pity from others.

CHAPTER 18

THE NON-LIMITATIONS OF HUMILITY

Humility is attainable for the normal person. It does not take an extraordinary, rule-following, holy human to attain humility. That was the hard part for me to learn. It took me years to realize that I could practice being humble even while I was flawed. In fact, for years I was turned off by living a righteous lifestyle because I felt like it had to be all or nothing. I felt like if I did not pray, go to church, eat healthy, abstain from alcohol, stop cursing, etc., then there was no point to even starting to try at all. I was overwhelmed by the idea of trying to be a good person. I felt like I needed to go all in, and the anxiety crippled me at first.

It took years of pondering on humility to realize all these rules I had in my mind, all these limitations, were just lies I believed in because as a child I was not presented with an attainable way to have a relationship with God. I was taught that it was all or nothing. So for a while, I chose nothing. I could not keep up with everything living a Christian life required. I lived in fear that if I were a "lukewarm" Christian, I would never make it to heaven. But I felt so broken. I felt like people who were good Christians were just born that way. I felt like I was never good at being "good." I felt like I couldn't stick with any sort of structure for long. My inner being *loathed* structure. I did not understand how people accomplished things. I believed I would never be good at anything. Everything I tried I failed at.

I failed so often because I tried everything out of my own will. I was not humble enough to let the universe do what it needed to do with me. I was living in fear and anxiety because I was grasping at the idea that I needed to "do more." I was sad and stressed because I felt like the mounting tasks that normal people seem to be able to accomplish were too hard for me. I felt stupid. I felt tired. I felt really, really sad. I drank my feelings away. And still, they came back every day.

My pride would not let me live in the present. My pride said, "You need to be good at something to be validated." My pride put my standards in an unrealistic place. My expectations were adopted from the many years of adults hammering them into me, but they were all scared and living bleak, unhappy lives. Why would I follow expectations of how to fulfill my life from adults who didn't even know fulfillment?

My pride took a big step back when I finally was like, "Wow, I don't know anything." Everything I thought I knew I slowly realized was untrue. I finally started to dissect it all. I decided to question everything I was taught and changed the way I thought and the way I rationalized. I was not going to be the same person I always was. I truly changed. A real change. A change that almost felt physical, like my DNA was swapped or something. My pride was kicked aside, and I was able to morph the way I thought and consider things that were blacklisted from my brain my whole life. I was able to question the very moral basis my whole foundation was built on.

I finally understood that God loved me just the way I was. That I was always walking with him. That even the fact I was concerned with what kind of Christian I was showed him I was devoted. I realized that I was right where I needed to be. I didn't have to be at church every Sunday or pray around the table at night before dinner for my relationship with him to matter more. What mattered was that I acknowledged my pride. What mattered was to always consider God in situations. And if I make the wrong choice, I always acknowledge that.

I was so focused on what a good life looked like that I couldn't focus on the present—just being with God and being okay with where I was in life. I used to think I needed to start drilling Bible verses into my head even to be considered good enough to be a missionary. I was so focused on the examples of all the people around me in my church that I felt I was not good enough.

I later realized I was made the way I am because I brought something so unique and niche to God's table. I was made extraordinary. I was made to do things different and test the waters.

I was made to be a person who questioned what I was told. I was made to question rules.

Why am I talking about my destiny, for lack of a better term? Because you cannot step into your destiny if you do not get rid of the pride that is holding you down in a mold that you were conditioned to stay in. You are partaking in standards created by people who basically don't know anything more about the meaning of life than you do. You are clueless; they are clueless. We are all wrong, probably about everything.

Admitting that you are clueless will do your life wonders. Just decide to stop arguing with every thought that tells you you're anxious about something. When you start to feel stress or sadness, immediately ask yourself why, and realize that the worst outcome from your situation is probably not as bad as you think. We are so concerned with ourselves and people's perceptions of us that we can never just be okay having someone see us making a mistake. If you are about to puke because you have to make a speech, it's because you are scared of looking stupid in front of people or being rejected by them in some way. That stuff is just our ego saying that we cannot seem socially lower than a certain level or else we will chemically combust. No! That's just not true. We are far too self-focused, and it robs us of our joy. It's robbing us of our peace.

Don't put too much faith in humanity to know what's good for you. That's between you and God.

What I am trying to make very clear is that this is something we can all do. Any average person can become self-aware. All you need to be self-aware is to notice your pride. Once you notice it and are able to map out the hurt it causes, then you start to figure out ways to weed it out on your own. Your whole being will recognize the virus and attack. You will start to hear words come out of your mouth that don't sound right anymore. You will notice how those words are condescending to someone else or yourself.

CHAPTER 19

HOW TO SURVIVE SOCIAL MEDIA

We live in fast times. Modern problems require modern solutions. Enter social media. What I want you to be able to do is coexist with it.

I wrote this book in 2020—a presidential election year. Facebook posts with political arguments or "conversations" are emerging. You believe very deeply in a certain social issue, and a so-called Facebook friend of yours does not. You start to have this "conversation," because why can't two mature adults talk about it? The conversation goes back and forth, nothing gets resolved, and you both end up thinking less of each other.

I see this happen over and over. It kills me. It's wasted time on everyone's part. I do think, yes, mature adults can surely talk about this stuff, but when it's taking over almost all your social media conversations, it's probably a good time to step back and ask who you are *really* trying to help. As people, we can be more concerned with being right than actually changing our opponent's mind. Something I learned is that it's really hard to change someone's mind. People will think what they want to, and the best way to lead is by example. Earn trust first, be a kind human, make a connection with someone, then lead them by example. I have had so many people preach to me, but they were never people I fully trusted or connected with in the first place, so there was little reason to listen to a word they said. They have never shown me true concern, only that they were zealous about their beliefs. What they believed was more important than how they treated me.

I bring up social media arguments because, in a modern world, they cause so much frustration. As I've mentioned, I once succumbed to debates on Facebook and realized after getting my heart hurt a few times that I was insane for even wasting my time and efforts this way.

I decided to cut that out as well. I wanted to be a good friend to all. I wanted to be a safe place for all, so I stopped centering my message on my opinions and beliefs. I didn't want people to think of those things when they thought of me; I wanted them to think of me as Jessica the artist who is fun to talk to and super helpful anytime they asked me a question. That's who I was created to be. Rather than be an opinionated asshat, I chose not to push people away. No internet argument is going to change the issues we face. Bringing awareness and education is not wrong, but focusing on kindness and love gains people's trust. Being humble enough to know the problem will not be solved through arguing solves issues because we work on our own hearts and our own intentions first. Many people preach to other people about how they could be a better human, and meanwhile the person preaching is a pretty awful friend, hasn't experienced emotional growth in years, and never truly grew up. I don't like to take advice from people who aren't always actively growing and working on themselves.

Modern-day humbleness has become quite complicated. Social media has made it possible to advertise all our thoughts and plaster them online at every chance. It has made it possible for everyone to have a voice. People criticize other people's body parts or reject people by stating "please unfriend me if you are _____." Once, my Facebook was hacked by my teenage nemesis. She posted lewd statuses that were so offensive, I dare not write them in this book.

We live in a new age, folks. Keep your passwords protected, and don't tell *anyone* the name of your first pet. The way I see it, we can cut out the noise of pride that rings out across all the platforms so you can still remain social, use these platforms, and save yourself from getting sucked into self-worship.

self-worship: extravagant admiration for or devotion to oneself: worship of oneself: SELF-IDOLATRY

On the internet, people try to become like God. We've all seen people posting perfectly angled selfies to celebrate feeling beautiful. I mean the whole deal. Every day. Their stories are silent, and there they are, gawking at the camera to show all their perfect, smooth features with the new filter they found. Doting on all their highlight reels. Never showing you the mess behind the scenes.

Posting selfies and celebrating wins does not make you a narcissist. If it did, I would be quite the hypocrite. But I also show people the real me. Even the raw, hard moments. The internet is a platform for people to put themselves, their photos, and their words on a pedestal in front of the world so other people can admire them without seeing their true identity. It's a world of insecure, self-centered people. People who feel like they can't measure up. People who are addicted to the instant gratification of likes and comments. It's also a world in which we feel less alone, but while using it, it's separating us from the thing that can actually cure loneliness. We are filling ourselves with a false sense of comfort when we tune out real life and only tune in to our world online.

This might all sound elementary and obvious. But is it? Maybe you don't really care for social media, or maybe you can think of a time where you used it to fill a gap of loneliness. Either way, social media is taking up most of the ways we communicate now, and it will only get bigger and bigger. We have to talk about this and be aware of it constantly. We have to know how to react when an issue on social media comes up and how to guard our heart from the hurt and rejection it can cause. We also have to be mindful of ourselves and how we use it. We need to be aware of when we could be projecting our negative feelings online. This is our world now, and while physical connection is king, I still believe we need to be careful what we put out into our cyberworld.

The thing here that's going to separate you from pride and humility is defining your "why." What is your purpose in posting those selfies and winning moments? If it's to show off, elicit jealousy, or show everyone that they are beneath you, then that's a very blatant show of pride. If it's because you're excited, you feel confident, or you want to bring some light into the world whether or not you get a ton of likes, or any at all, then that's humility. If we are so dependent on likes and social media love, then we are missing out on life entirely. Our fulfilment can't come from online feedback or the amount of social media attention we get. It shouldn't be breaking people down the way it does. If social media is hurting you, then it has too much power over you.

My favorite speaker and author who talks about social media while also being wildly humble is the incredible Gary Vaynerchuk (or, as he often goes by, Gary Vee). For those of you who don't know him, he is one of the most successful entrepreneurs of our generation, dedicated to teaching everything he knows to anyone who will listen. Even though he is considered social media royalty with large followings on all platforms, he avidly speaks about humility, empathy, and kindness. Almost obsessively.

In December 2018, I went to a business seminar with my mom to see Tony Robbins. At the time, I was new to the self-help world and hadn't heard of the other speakers in Tony's lineup, which included Gary. When Gary got onstage, I was immediately drawn in. It's hard to ignore someone saying "fuck" more times than I've been told "I love you" in my life. Here's a young-at-heart dude who talks about social media as the key to business. He said one thing every other speaker overlooked: that we must use social media in an authentic, empathetic way. Most other speakers were older. Some of their advice did not apply to modern business. Gary Vee was so transparent. Without having gone to that conference and learning who he was, I'm not sure I would be writing this right now.

Over and over, Gary Vee used the words "kindness," "humility," and "empathy." *Okay, Gary*, I thought, *I get it. Be nice, and don't be an asshat. Easy.* But over the years, his message never changed. He said it again and again and again. Two years into listening to Gary Vee podcasts, I finally felt his message click. I learned what it meant to be empathic and humble on social media. I learned how to be kind by not reacting irrationally toward something upsetting I read from a friend. I also learned how to refrain from adding negativity to the world.

Gary Vee's advice made me realize how most social media posts by other businesses were just empty words. They sounded great but didn't empathize with the customer or their needs. For example, let's say you own an earring company, and in the caption of a photo you post on social media, you write, "Who doesn't love and deserve these cute earrings? Treat yourself!" For one, maybe the person seeing the earrings doesn't love them. Maybe they've been a bad girl (or boy) and don't deserve to treat themselves for a hot minute because they spent $350 dollars at Target on pillows.

In that example, you can tell the company is posting on autopilot. It's inauthentic and ill-conceived. Business owners have to be specific or we start to sound boring and salesy. We have to show the value of what we are selling and not put together a bunch of empty phrases that don't show that we're trying to meet our viewers' needs. Ego-driven social media is about us and not so much the consumers. Something along the lines of this would be more helpful: "Check out our gold-plated hypoallergenic hoops. We call these our power hoops because they are big and bold. Wearing them might just give you that extra punch you need to rock out your outfit." This will help a customer visualize themselves using your product and will spread your passion for the product because it's genuine.

That was an example for businesses on social media, but what if you don't have a business but are trying to grow your social media following? How do you remain empathetic and humble on social media? It's simpler than you think. Be real about what's going on with you. Post your highs and lows. "My garden, which I worked so hard on, got overgrown with weeds. Keep watching my story to see my progress on how I fix it up." Or create a story or caption that outlines something you learned that helped you. Keep talking about whatever it is you're passionate about and don't stop. If you're truly passionate about it, it will come off as genuine because you won't be faking it. Something you don't want to post if you're trying to grow an online presence is, "Stay on your grind all day," or something cheesy like that. You need real depth. That's why I started to show up fully as myself. The real me. I felt like I had freedom on social media. I felt equipped to use it to my benefit, not tread water every time I logged on. Sometimes you need to hear the message over and over until you know what it feels like to live that message.

I heard what Gary said, but it took me years to understand how to live it. That is, how to walk with a humble heart. Many lessons may be heard but not understood right away. You need to constantly entertain the lifestyle of humility. Always acknowledge it. Eventually, it will lead you to humble pastures—that's where you want to be. I can say this because I've gotten myself lost in the pride of social media.

I was a keyboard warrior once. Always commenting on things I disagreed with for the sake of whatever cause I was defending. Always posting articles and statuses about my totally profound opinions that nobody had ever heard of before (sarcasm) in hopes that I would sound smart, show people how wrong they were, or hopefully get some comments from people agreeing with me because I was hoping for an echo-chamber audience to back me up. I lost friends, I made enemies, all because I thought blurting your opinion was how you helped the world be better.

I took a step back a while ago. I started to get really sick of feeling exhausted going back and forth with people. I asked myself, *Was this all worth it? Did I change anyone's mind with my one million posts? Or did I cause myself more problems?* The answer is that I was being a huge asshole. I realized the real way to change the minds of those around me and get people to side with what I was passionate about was to just show them kindness and be a friend. You can't earn the trust of those around you if you are always just being loud and over the top. And if you want people to listen, you need their trust. You need to show that they are in a safe place with you. People won't feel safe with you if they see you are always causing a ruckus on the interwebs. It's not humble to always insert your opinion.

Listen, the world will disappoint you. People will disappoint you. The humble thing to do is to realize you are going to be disappointed, not always agreed with, and sometimes will even stand alone. The humble thing is to know that being the loudest on the internet will not win over true love and kindness. Love people hard! That is how you bring all your passions to fruition and make a real statement. What cost are you willing to risk in order to "be right" on social media? Do you feel drained, upset, heated, or stressed after a keyboard warrior battle over the latest Kanye West drama? If the answer is yes, then you have a problem you need to cut out of your life. Even if the answer is not yes, please don't waste your day with that small-time shit. You are bigger than that. You are better than that. You are humble, and you are proud just to be you. That's what makes you honorable. That's what makes you strong. That's what makes you a leader. Don't stoop down to the tabloid-level arguments. If you can't help yourself and your blood boils when you read certain people's posts, then unfollow them. Please, for the love of God and your sanity (and everyone else's), just fucking unfollow them. Right now.

Actually, right now as you read this, I am telling you to take out your phone or your computer and unfollow, hide, unfriend, block, or do whatever you need to do in order to cut out the noise that is hurting you and causing you stress. Social media should never have control over you, but if it does, cut out what is draining you. I suggest the hide feature because I still love my friends. I do. But some of them truly drain me. I want to continue to love them, but in order to love them without resentment, I need to tune out their social media posts. I don't want to be upset when I see their posts, so the best way to love them is to hide what I see. If you can't hide them, then you might have to make the hard decision to unfriend and be ready to be confronted about it and be prepared with a heartfelt and vulnerable response.

It's hard, but social media should not be stealing your joy. It should not be controlling you; it should not be more important than the things in front of you. I am always on social media, talking, posting photos, and interacting. But when I start to feel a little too into it, I know to step away. I go outside with my kids, drink some coffee, and live in the moment. It has been especially hard for me because being on social media is part of my job, since it's pretty much how I make my money. Here are some tips to have a healthy balance:

- If you are on your phone and someone is talking to you, ask for a minute to finish up, but give them your full attention when you're done. Or put it down right away and pay attention. But don't give half-assed attention.
- Set realistic expectations. Sometimes you will see things that irk you, but make a conscious decision beforehand not to entertain or engage.
- Don't entertain or engage in bullshit.
- Post things for the right reason, not because you want them to boost your ego.
- Turn it off if it's draining you.
- Hide, block, or unfriend people who truly cause more harm than good, if you really cannot ignore them on your own.

Trust me, friends, I'm still guilty of these social media sins. Sometimes I entertain things I shouldn't or allow my feedback on social media to boost me up. We all do. It's a big devil that takes practice to conquer. The biggest thing here is to recognize when we are feeling off because of something we participated in or read on social media. We need to be aware of the emotions that social media evokes in us and how to spot it as it's happening and step back before we become overtaken by it. Outrage and offense is a sin. If you aren't religious, we will just call it bad. It's wrong, it's flat-out wrong. Yes, we will feel outrage and offense, but we are not being forgiving and understanding if we are acting out on it. Those emotions are from a place of pride. Humility would forgive and realize it's our unrealistic expectations telling us we deserve something else other than whatever it is we are being offended by. Just because someone has given you a reason to defend yourself or react doesn't mean you should. Taking the high road is the hardest road. But it's also the only road with a reward at the end. Which is the best award in life, obviously.

Lastly, even if you do everything right online, you're still going to have haters. Even Jesus, who was said to have walked the earth as a perfect human being, had haters! So many, in fact, that they crucified him. If people will crucify a perfect man, then they will for sure crucify your ass. It's human nature to turn on your own every once in a while. All you can do is control yourself. Control your reactions and your heart. Guard your heart the best you can, but when these things spring up on a casual Monday when you are just trying to scroll in peace, be ready to forgive and tune out the noise.

CHAPTER 20

LETTING GO OF CONTROL

If you haven't noticed, I have had an ongoing standoff with control. I always seem to be fighting God for it. The harder I fight, the less I control. I was fighting with God for years over my internal happiness. After I became pregnant with my first son, I reformed a little bit and tried to become a real contributing adult, but it was not at all what I thought it would be. I was trying to physically practice happiness by doing things I saw happy people doing. Working myself to the bone by doing good things for myself thinking somehow the more work I put in, the more real joy it would bring.

I ended up being even more sad because nothing I did was ever enough. Never clean enough, never eating healthy enough, never taking my kids to the park enough, going to church enough, talking to my friends enough. I was trying so hard to control my way of life in a physical way that I never dug into my heart to see what was really holding me back. I was scared of the universe just doing its thing. I was scared that anything could happen to me at any given second. I thought if I did all the things someone who seems to be in control does, then that would make me in control and happy.

I was sorely mistaken when I thought doing all those things would put me in control or make me happy. It left me so empty. I felt like I was broken because I couldn't do normal things most people seemed to be able to do, like have a daily routine. But how come all these other happy people were able to do these things daily? I thought a routine would bring happiness—that must be what I was missing, right? Not at all. I later realized that happiness comes before routine. How the shit am I going to wake up, go for a run, make a green smoothie, and write my mantras of thankfulness if I'm not happy? I could not even roll out of bed. I loathed waking up to do life. I didn't even care to eat anymore. That's how sad I was. I lost so much weight because I was hardly even there, just doing the minimum of what I needed to do to survive my day.

I know this sounds really lame, but I went on a spiritual journey. It took years of self-reflecting, dissecting, looking at who I really was. I had to look at my faults, my strengths, my triggers, and my distractions. I had to let go of the idea that I could somehow control happiness into my life. That happiness equaled more work. Happiness felt unattainable because I was attaching it to the idea that I needed to work for it. But the joy comes first, and then the other stuff follows because the happiness is already there. All of a sudden, I have energy when I wake up. I want to make a delicious smoothie; I want to clean my house and actually be awake rather than wondering when I can drink a whole bottle of wine. I let go of the control. I decided that those things just weren't going to happen. I let go of the stress to get them done. I felt a weight lift off my shoulders when I decided that I just wasn't going to do that stuff, like *at all*. I was not going to put any more pressure on myself to control my situation. My stress literally vanished when I let go of it. I decided things just need to happen the way they need to happen.

Once I fixed the journey from the inside out, the outside things started happening. You don't have to change your whole life in a physical way to change your whole life. I made the choice to start on the inside, because something in my brain seriously needed some growth. I have seen over and over people trying so hard to create happiness by doing whatever the new happiness is, then they just fall back into feeling the same emptiness again.

I give you permission to just stop. Don't give in to the pressure that you need to operate how you see other people operating. I felt so much pressure as an adult seeing what other adults were doing with their lives. I didn't have my shit together for years, and it stressed me out because I felt so inadequate and like a dirt human for not being able to do what most normal people could do. I felt like I must have been the lowest of the low. Completely unable to do a normal task without feeling overwhelmed.

The truth is, most adults start out pretending to know how this all works, but all of us have our dirty little secret we are ashamed to admit about our daily lives. When I was speaking to my psychiatrist about some personal problems, she asked me if I would feel ashamed if anyone knew these things about me. I said yes, of course. That was my biggest fear—that people would see how fully out of control I really was. Like how could I be contributing to society as a human if I could not get this personal problem in control? She kind of laughed and said that everyone who comes into her office talking about personal stuff always feels this way. That generally everyone has a secret they are ashamed to admit and that compared to most people, I was actually one of her more normal clients. It showed my shame in a new light. That I truly was not alone. That, in honesty, humans are still animals. I was trying to hide myself so hard that I didn't even want to show a human and raw form of myself, and that was pretty natural.

Do I want to use this book to talk about something I have kept so secret? The answer is no. I'm going to write it, but I might delete this whole part and never share it. I just feel like writing it down will help me let go of the shame a little. I have OCD that presents itself through dermatillomania, which is an obsessive skin-picking disorder. Now, you would not know that by looking at my face, because I honestly am pretty good at not overpicking my face, but I pick parts of my body that I can easily hide. I always had the tick, but over the past five years, it grew into something I couldn't control anymore. I usually spend hours a day picking at seemingly nothing. I can't wear certain clothes because it shows, and I don't want to have the awkward conversation, "I'm obsessed with picking my skin. What's your most terrifying secret?" I have hundreds, if not thousands, of pick marks all over me. Somehow I can quit drinking cold turkey, but I can't quit this, at least not yet. It's been a work in progress. It really had me bummed out. I didn't understand how I could have anything of strength and value to offer anyone when I couldn't even get this under control. I have all this confidence on how to make my life better, go after my dreams, and let go of control, yet I can't stop this tick that's ruining my self-image.

Control. I won't have it, and it won't have me. I won't let it tell me I'm not worthy or don't have strength because of my shameful faults. Here I am telling the world my biggest shame because if I talk about humility, I better walk it. Some of you are probably reading and are like, "*Pshhh*, is that all you got?" I know I'm not alone. I know there are others with much deeper shames, and the idea that we have control of this monster is just not true. Your shame can't stop you from being strong and valuable. You might feel gross from your shame, but that is just fear lying to you, telling you that if you are found out people will be just as disgusted as you are with yourself. Everyone has a secret shame. You don't have to tell the world about it like I did. But don't let it own you; own it and throw it in the trash. Live your life despite it and keep going forward. Don't let the things you feel are inadequate about yourself run the way you live your life. We are literally just flesh and bones with a big, mushy brain. We aren't all that and a bag of chips, okay? You're allowed to have flaws, even if you think they are weird or gross. On the inside we are still just a bunch of blood and guts, not gods!

So there you have it. My secret. I just want to make it clear how absolutely flawed I am. Anyone teaching about self-help, business, and happiness might seem like they have it all together. See, I don't like that. Where is the humility in that? I don't want to teach about unattainable heights. I want to show you that humility and joy in your life is a weird road. That sometimes it's time to shed light on the darkness. You need to recognize your imperfections and decide even with these things, you will keep going, while still acknowledging they are there. Maybe even confine your secret to a trusted person. Really open up and explain why you feel so much shame from it. The reason this will heal you better is because you are unloading a huge burden of a secret. Also, we as humans are afraid to admit our humanness sometimes. It's okay to show that we have gotten dirty. It's truly humbling. That is a big outward move toward humility. Being vulnerable with our shame. Shedding light on it. Not only will you start a journey to heal your heart, but it's also saying a big fuck you to feeling ashamed. Unload your hurting heart. Just please be sure to do it with a very trustworthy friend, spouse, or family member, or go to a licensed therapist, which I have done, and it gave me so much insight!

Letting go of control is about losing the expectation that things must go any which way we try to steer them. Inevitably, we get a rude awakening when we find our efforts at control are not met when the situation goes absolutely sideways. The idea that we are in control of anything will absolutely eventually disappoint us. Once we decide to understand that we cannot force ourselves into happiness and fulfillment is when we actually obtain happiness and fulfilment.

Now, certain things you can take control of. But don't be in such a deep battle of control that when you lose what you were trying to grasp, you get completely disappointed and hurt. Because obviously, I would have not been able to stop drinking alcohol without some form of control over myself. I'm not saying don't attempt control at anything. This is more of an inner battle. A battle over our expectations and what we think should happen to us versus what actually ends up happening. I have a hard time with my OCD. Yes, I need to practice self-control, but also, I am not going to let that situation steal my joy. I won't keep myself under its control of shame. Shame is just fear. Fear that our hidden parts will be discovered. Fear of being humiliated. I humiliated my shame before it could humiliate me.

Now that we have an idea of how we try to control and silence ourselves, let's talk about how we try to control and silence other people. For me, it wasn't until about a year ago that I really decided to step back and be super patient when I dealt with people who I felt were hard to get along with. It's like having a drug addict family member. You try over and over to help them by getting them out of bad situations or talking them through what is ruining their lives and the lives of the ones they love. Yet they still keep relapsing and going back into old habits even though you felt you gave them every tool to claw themselves out. You grow upset, bitter, and hurt. You start to say nasty things to them, and you get a pit in your stomach even when they come to mind. You are just so mad they have been so selfish and reckless. It boggles your mind. This happens when you try to control anything but it was never yours to control in the first place. Sometimes, you have to learn to embrace the things you cannot control. Love the drug addict anyway. Let go of the idea that you can control and save anybody.

Let go of the idea that you will get what you want out of someone or that they will listen to your advice. Love deeply even if they continue to hurt you. Love so hard that you can let them go and still walk with forgiveness and empathy in your heart. We can still have empathy toward the most hardened of humans. We need to practice real, unrelenting love even when relationships, communities, and political agendas don't go our way. We need to offer unrelenting love to the people who hate us the most. And I mean real love. Inside and out. Slow to react and quick to listen. Slow to defend ourselves and quick to bring comfort.

We get so bitter and angry when we find ourselves in a tough situation with a friendship going south or your presidential candidate not getting elected. We are not in control. Things will happen that you won't like, over and over. Being patient and providing kindness, even when it seems impossible and you are not receiving that kindness back, is in fact the most honorable way of living. Deciding over and over, even when your heart is beaten down and you're rejected by people, that you will love anyway, even if those people want you dead, is in fact what it means to let go of control and live free. People who try to take control of things that seem out of control might react with eye rolls instead of eye contact. Defensiveness instead of comfort. Or getting loud instead of listening. It's uncomfortable as hell to feel out of control, but leaving your heart in a place of rest rather than a place of fury is going to serve you in a much bigger way. You cannot silence people; you cannot make the noise stop. The more you try to stop all the noise, the louder it gets. It was only when I became patient with people that living in a world filled with things I don't like became so much easier.

CHAPTER 21

CUTTING OUT THE NOISE

The noise. It's everywhere. When I say noise, I mean all the words, songs, TV shows, entertainment, news, and podcasts being ingested at all times. In our modern age, it's impossible to ignore all the noise. We're always consuming information, even when we don't realize it. I think we do it so often that we don't even stop to think about how our lives would be different if we stopped all the noise, even for a few days. What would it truly be like to turn it all off and not know what is happening in the world around us? To turn off all the things we mindlessly like to indulge in and just live in the now and soak in what is really going on with a clear mind?

Since deciding to quit drinking and remain sober, I have faced the so-called noise head-on. My biggest vice, alcohol, is no longer in my life to help me dull my senses to the noise, and I am left to deal with it in a very sober reality that I'm still trying to get used to. This is the longest I have been sober since I was thirteen years old. So life still feels strange without something to indulge in and use to help alleviate my mind of this constantly yapping world. In order to become the best version of yourself, you need to know what it's like to live without numbing your senses. You need to take a step back with a sober mind, turn off the music, the movies, the podcasts, and really see yourself for who you are. You need to take a few days or a few weeks to know what it's like to disconnect from the world and truly not know what's going on. No more news or social media, just you and your head. Once you get in this space of clearness, you can really start to dissect who you are, what you love, and what has been making you feel icky.

Music was always a big part of my life. I grew up going to local hardcore and punk rock shows. Listening to loud angsty music every weekend. Hanging out with my edgy and super-sad angsty friends. All my favorite memories growing up were with these people, hanging out after shows and going on mindless adventures. So as I grew up, listening to music continued to be a huge part of my life. Years later, I was still listening to the same bands and a few new ones. But like any edgy music snob, I felt a band's first album was just so much cooler than their new stuff, dude. It took me years and years of listening to music to realize something: music was not that great for me. It turns out, listening to songs about how out of your mind you are can sort of make you feel out of your mind. I realized after listening to music on long car rides that I often felt too sad, too hyped up, or too self-absorbed.

Let me explain. I'm not a person who thinks I'm a big bad bitch who is independent and doesn't need no man. But when I listen to Cardi B, I sure as shit do. And when I listen to Cardi B for two hours during a long car ride, I pop out of that car feeling like I just made a million dollars and I have to pay my mama's bills because I don't have time to chill, okurrrrr. I strut into my house like I own the place, which I do, high off my car ride jam sesh, and start complaining to my husband about not hustling with taking out the trash while I was gone. A strong, independent woman shouldn't have to remind you twice, okurrrrr? I'm trying to pay my mama's bills, Jeff. I don't have time to chill or have time to wait for the trash to be taken out. I start snapping my fingers, demanding that shit get done. I turn into a real peach, to say the least.

That was a more lighthearted example, but this kind of stuff happens. When you soak in music and entertainment, it really molds your mind so that the emotions of others become a theme in your life. When I listened to emo music, I realized my soul felt exhausted and emotional afterward. I would listen to rap and hip hop and feel larger than life. Music changed my state of mind. I listened to certain music depending on how I wanted to feel. I used it as a crutch to cut out the noise of whatever I was actually feeling, to create a new temporary emotion to cover up my sobering reality.

I think we do this so often and don't realize how we use music and entertainment to cover up what we really feel. It is happening all day, all around us. People tend to want to surround themselves with an echo chamber of noise that will reinforce their state of mind and be in agreement with how they want to feel. Like someone who is going through a breakup—they don't want to feel the real emotions of loss and instead want to feel like they are saying, "C'ya never. I'm too good for you anyways." Then they turn on some empowering breakup song to alter their natural state. We have to learn to work within these states with a sober and clear mind. To really know what they feel like and work through them with no crutches and allow ourselves to feel all the emotions, even if they aren't good ones. We cannot tune out what is really going on inside us. We have to tune in by cutting the noise out.

Once I realized music played a huge role in some of my negative emotions, I decided to stop listening to it as much. Now, some people would say music helps them focus or relax, but even then, what is it about a quiet place that makes it hard to focus or relax? Could it be that focusing has always been hard, and maybe there is a reason for it that is much deeper? Could you have a lot of stress, and that's why relaxing is so hard? We have to ask ourselves these questions. Sometimes we have to get really quiet to truly hear what is going on inside us. To really see what we are hiding with all the noise. Why do we feel the need to numb our thoughts so often with entertainment?

I'm not saying listening to music is bad. But we all do this stuff. It's happening to all of us all the time, and if it's never brought up and you truly don't get real about what is going on in your heart, then you can't ever see what is holding you back. Part of being humble is being soberly self-aware. Being able to dissect the real you—who you are when all the lights are out and the noise is gone. What is stressing you? What is making you happy? What is scaring you? This will help you nail down your why. Why you strive for greatness and where your pride could be hiding.

Music was distracting me big-time, and I didn't realize how much it was until I stopped drinking. Once I stopped drinking alcohol, I saw a buttload of things I was using as an outlet, things that hindered me from dealing with my issues. I was unable to even focus on my goals because of these things.

I made a conscious decision to start soaking business-related information in place of music. I needed a big mindset change, and I didn't know where to start. But I knew if I listened to some audiobooks and podcasts, it could help me work through the stuff I was hiding. I ended up listening to twenty books in twelve months and dozens of entrepreneurship podcast episodes. It completely transformed my mind and changed me as a human. All because I cut out music and replaced it with tangible information on how to work through what it means to be happy and successful, the real way, not the overly hyped-up way. The slow and steady way.

Can books and podcasts also be distracting? Of course, but I decided to clear my mind and concentrate on these things with absolute laser focus. I cut out alcohol and most of my music to solely focus on my dreams and work on finding real happiness. In a small amount of time, it worked. Now when I listen to a lot of music, I am able to realize that I'm in an unhealthy place, and I step back and ask myself why. Being self-aware is knowing what it is you resort to when you are having inner issues so that you can recognize it quickly, assess what is going on, and deal with it. Basically my whole life, until just recently, I never knew I used music for this reason. Whatever you listen to is what your mind attaches to. You are essentially feeding your soul whatever type of entertainment you are consuming. If you are constantly watching quirky love-story movies, then you probably will start to feel like you are in a quirky love story. Or if you keep listening to conspiracy-theory documentaries, you will eventually become convinced birds aren't real and are actually government drones.

Excessive entertainment is used as a crutch. Alcohol was my main squeeze. But after cutting it out, I realized I also relied on music too much. Anything in excess is generally something we are using to cover up something else. I drink excessive amounts of coffee now. I traded my alcohol habit for a new habit. Two to four cups of coffee a day. All day. Lately I've even started drinking coffee at 9:00 p.m. I have become self-aware enough to realize that coffee is my new crutch. I'm often tired because I have a hard time sleeping, and I have a hard time sleeping because I'm stressed, and I'm stressed because I am not great at organizing my time and my day. All day is work time for me. If I could address the issue of lowering my stress, I would probably get more sleep and not rely on coffee so much.

My goal is to eventually lack nothing. What I mean by that is I don't want to have any forms of entertainment or indulgences that I feel I depend on. I want to be content with just myself without feeling like I need to indulge in anything for that instant gratification feeling.

CHAPTER 22

VULNERABILITY

A few weeks ago I was sitting in my therapist's office, holding back tears because I didn't feel comfortable crying in front of a person I had only met a handful of times. I was terrified of what she thought of me aside from her "professional" welcoming feeling that I assume all therapists try to portray. I was wondering if I was a client that she would go home and talk about to her spouse and complain I sounded bratty or that my problems were minuscule. I was afraid I was really not cared for by her at all and she only listened because it was her job. I held back tears because I felt like my emotional vulnerability might not be met with the same vulnerability. After all, this was not a friendship; this was a professional relationship for her.

She saw that my voice was breaking as I tried to explain my hurt. She asked, "Why is it hard to cry in front of me?" I explained I felt very vulnerable and it was uncomfortable to cry in front of people I wasn't super close with. She kept asking me more questions to get deep down to see why it bothered me so much. Was I afraid of being rejected? Was I afraid of looking foolish? I answered her questions, pretty much yes to all of the above. She asked, "Is it pride stopping you from being vulnerable?" I'm not sure what I said after that point, but she broke down my walls, and I eventually started bawling my eyes out. I kept apologizing, and she kept telling me not to apologize for being emotional. I told her about all the hurt and fear of rejection. My pride was protecting me from becoming vulnerable and then getting rejected for being vulnerable. It dawned on me that I kept up this tough front and attitude because I was so terrified of people knowing I had a weakness. My pride wanted to portray me as stronger than I was. My fear was being rejected for being vulnerable.

I was opened to a new world of pride that I had been living in. I knew I did this to an extent, but I didn't realize it was so obvious. At some point in this tearful meeting, we broached the subject of religion. She found out I was a Christian and she was as well. She asked if she could pray for me. I said yes. I felt comforted by her prayer but also felt uncomfortable. Prayer is a vulnerable thing, and I so badly wanted to be in that vulnerable spiritual place with someone, but I was so scared of it being taken away or people seeing me for the hurt person I was. But it showed me she was willing to be vulnerable with me. She made clear that this was not just her job but that she was truly attempting to connect and help me. Our twenty-minute meeting turned into an hourlong meeting. I left feeling a little naked, knowing I shared my emotions but also that not everyone will reject my vulnerability.

This meeting moved me to a place of contemplation. I couldn't stop thinking about it; it was a breakthrough of some sort. I realized I had a really hard time talking about my true feelings to anybody, and it had been hurting all my relationships. I realized I felt wildly uncomfortable being vulnerable with people, especially my family. But mostly, with myself. The idea of even admitting I had a lot of enduring hurt threw me off course. I had been ignoring the little girl inside me that had been hurting since childhood. Having never really mended those pains, I'd instead cemented them shut and moved on. The idea of even taking the time to acknowledge those things, deal with them, and fix those relationships sounded way too uncomfortable. In addition, I honestly didn't want to waste my time getting emotional when I could work instead, or watch Netflix, eat food, or sleep. Anything but talk about emotional stuff.

What is sort of sad is I fantasize about being emotional and vulnerable with my feelings. I want badly to talk about them freely and admit my hurt. I literally daydream of being myself but can never quite do it because I have too much pride in this persona I've created. I have spent so many years trying to shield myself from hurt. I spent years believing, truly believing, that I was stupid and annoying. To the point where I thought my IQ must be so low that I could never amount to anything because I just wasn't capable. I felt inadequate because I got bored so quickly and was uninterested in things most people find normal. I cannot believe I convinced myself I was truly so much less than other people. I was vulnerable with the wrong people, and their words convinced me I was all wrong. Any group of friends I tried to join eventually made me feel too much. I am a super-sensitive person, who is also relentless. So my strong personality often was met with pushback. I just felt so much shame in who I was. I had no self-esteem in my capabilities. I assumed everything I said was irritatingly obvious, and people were not interested in hearing me talk.

Once I started photography and became a mother, I completely reenvisioned what I thought of myself. I was suddenly capable of so much. I realized I was different because I was extraordinary. I was destined to go down a different path than most. I was meant to stand alone during most of my journey and learn things completely on my own. I started to see I was able to surpass what people around me were doing. I did a whole lifetime of growth within a few short years. I was learning things I saw people in old age still struggling with. My mind was freed of most of the old lies I told myself. I, in fact, was not stupid. I was capable and actually quite intelligent. I don't mean this in a bragging way. What I mean is that I rewrote all these lies I had believed. I rewrote who I was. I stepped into the truth of who I was and was able to harness a hidden power that I believe we all have. My strength is being able to see what is not working and pivot to something that does. And I do it quickly. I feel like I am in a rush to grow. And maybe I am. I hate sitting still, and I need to move. I started climbing faster than I've ever climbed. The frenzy to personal growth has consumed me ever since the first bite. I became a doer. I had never been a doer—then one day, I just was. Once the doing started, it never stopped.

Now even through all this doing, I had a major crisis of pride that I didn't see. Even though I'd moved away from those problems of rejection and hurt, I still never dealt with them. I blanketed them with a tough attitude and the idea that since I was a mom now, I just wouldn't have close friends anymore. Problem solved! I was getting rid of friends, so there was no need to deal with those issues.

Wrong! The child in me still begs to come out and experience love in all forms. Through friendships, in a deeper marriage, from my family members and children. I need to allow these relationships to be in my life, on a deep level, in order to be an actual strong person. Strength is vulnerability. Humility is not shielding yourself from the world. Humility is being who you were meant to be. All the parts.

Even the parts you don't like. Pride does not want to show the parts of us that make us feel shame. Like my dermatillomania.

It's funny. My therapist also asked, "What is the worst thing that will happen if people find out about your skin picking? What are you so afraid of?" I told her I'm scared of people thinking I'm gross or that I have a disorder. She then asked, "But what about them thinking it looks weird really bothers you? Why is that so terrible?" The answer was pride. Pride that I didn't want to admit my shame to them. Pride that I didn't want to show myself, raw and human. I no longer allow myself to live within the confines of shame and humiliation as I once did.

I say all this about myself because I feel it's very relatable. This is what I've learned on my journey, and I hope it can bring some comfort and insight to those with these same struggles.

CHAPTER 23

YOUR PLACE OF PEACE

I feel like my whole life I have been on a quest for peace. It has actually brought me a lot of stress. Here's an example. My stress level is really high when my boys argue with each other or when they scream and run in the house and everything seems like chaos. When you have three boys, that is basically all the time. I wait all day until they go to bed and I can finally get some peace and quiet. I put them to bed, and I feel the knot that was in my stomach all day just disappear. Ah yes, finally! I can sit in silence with nobody needing anything from me.

About three minutes into this moment of peace, I hear the footsteps of my youngest son. I can tell they are his footsteps because he stomps when he walks. He asks for a cup of water, which by the way I don't even think he drinks. My stomach tightens up again knowing my moment of peace has been interrupted and I have to get this kiddo some water. I get him the cup and he's off to bed. I sit back down and can finally relax. Five minutes later I hear my other son yell, "Mommy! Come here!" I let out an annoyed sigh and go to his room. He proceeds to ask me, "Mommy, are crabs a part of the spider family?" For a six-year-old, he asks pretty inquisitive questions. I try to answer the best I can to explain the difference, but I generally make up an explanation because there possibly is some correlation between crabs and spiders, but I'm not sure what it is.

I finally go back onto the couch to answer some emails in peace. Well, it turns out my kids had a whole other idea. They interrupt my peaceful flow about another seven times, and every time it gets interrupted, the knot in my stomach gets tighter, and I wonder if I will even get a chance to pay attention to the work in front of me at all this evening. By the time the kids are officially in bed and asleep, I'm exhausted from all the back and forth, and I'm unmotivated to pay attention to the task I had been waiting all day to do.

All day I search for peace. And every day I'm disappointed because it's never quite reached. My thoughts never stop. There is never a time when there are no tasks on my mental to-do list. I realize I have lost my peace in the quest of trying to gain peace. I tread water every day toward it. Looking back now, it's been a life struggle of mine. Always waiting for a break and never getting one. Always waiting to rest but never feeling comfortable. Not only that, but I realize it's a big problem with most people. Especially people who deal with anxiety like me.

Growing up, I remember my mom always looking for a break or a time of peace but never getting it. I remembered her constant quest for a mental break would stress everyone out. It was obvious she was anxious. Loud noise irritated her, questions irritated her, and the work that seemed to pile up irritated her. Her mental to-do list was never complete, and I feel like once I became an adult, I inherited this same anxiety. I always felt like anything I did wasn't enough, and my to-do list grew by the day. I keep notes in my phone of things I need to do, and it looks a little like this: get lightbulb, vacuum both cars, get stains out of marble countertops, organize garage, organize closet, finish redecorating, paint the kids' room, clean the bathtub, weed the garden, replant the garden, make content, post on social media, mend that one dress that doesn't fit right, etc. It goes on and on, and I'm dreading all those tasks because I feel like I don't have the time or motivation to do them. I also have to take a break to try and eat during my daily stress crisis, and the food is generally not enjoyable because I am too stressed to even savor it. Story of my life.

This all has me thinking, Why am I like this? Why do I lose so much peace? Will I ever make it to a place of inner rest?

I came up with two issues that could potentially be causing me to lose my peace.

1. The first one is procrastination. I notice sometimes when we get overwhelmed, we tend to clam up and put off the task that is causing us anxiety. I mean, why wouldn't we? It's a natural response to confrontation. It's a natural response to something that makes us feel uncomfortable. Working on tasks that require actual work doesn't sound as appealing as literally relaxing and doing anything else but those tasks. But after we put it off, we are left even more stressed than before because we didn't get it done in a timely manner. I was attending a business workshop in 2018. Something one of the speaker's said really stuck with me: procrastination is selfish. I had to think about it because at first it didn't make sense. But when I thought back to all the times procrastination stole my peace and all the times I was emotionally checked out during time with my family because I was thinking about all the work piling up that I needed to do because I had procrastinated all week, I realized just how selfish it was that I couldn't be emotionally available to them. It truly stole my joy, and if I had done what I needed to do in the first place, I would not have had to worry so much when I was trying to have family time. I needed to finish the tasks that would cause me stress so I could be clear and lighthearted when I was with my kids. So I could actually enjoy my time with them instead of stressing about all

the work that needed to get done. When I actually tackle the things I would usually procrastinate over, sleeping at night is so much easier. My mind doesn't need to continually remind me of my to-do list, because it's already done. This even applies to confrontation. If you need to confront someone but the idea is stressing you out, just do it as quickly as possible, once you have collected your thoughts. Rip off the Band-Aid. You can literally make yourself physically ill by stewing over the anxiety of confrontation.

2. The second reason I lose my peace is because my heart around the idea of anxiety is wrong. Prolonged anxiety and worry is almost a sin. To live in perpetual fear is not what God wants us to focus on. Worrying and being fearful can be unlearned. We can rewrite the lies that convince us we are anxious all the time. We have to dig deep and ask why we are really so worried. What is really the worst thing that can happen? I always rework an anxiety-causing situation in my head to try to step back and imagine the worst. More times than not, my situation is never as scary as I thought. In the past, I used to stress a lot about money and having none. I was afraid of scarcity. I had to step back and really look at what the worst thing would be if we lost all our money. The answer was never that bad, yet I lost so much sleep over the idea of losing it. I'm not saying certain instances are not bad, but our daily worries are typically quite minuscule in comparison to how bad things could really get.

My worst-case scenario was this: What if we didn't have enough money to pay rent and got kicked out? My husband and I both had parents who lived close by, and if something ever happened, we could have moved in with one of them. In 2016, we bought a house. Six months later, lightning struck a tree in our front yard, shaking the whole home and breaking the pipes underneath our house. The cost to fix the foundation was almost half of what the house cost, and we just could not afford it. With no running water, my husband, our three kids, and I had to move in with my husband's mother, bless her heart for taking us in. We lived there for half a year. For us, that was our worst-case scenario, and honestly, it wasn't that bad. We were a little cramped, but it was a fun time, and I got to know my mother-in-law better. We did lose the home and had to sell it because insurance would not cover repairs for us, but honestly, it was the best thing that ever happened to us. My heart during that time totally changed. I think that's when I started to truly trust the process and stopped stressing over money. After that whole ordeal, my mind changed toward money. Because we physically went through the worst-case scenario, I was able to see it wasn't really that bad and I stopped losing sleep over money, for the most part. (Though I have to admit, anytime I invested in my business more I did freak out a little.)

Want to hear something crazy? Since our insurance would not cover the damage to our home, we actually got referred to an attorney who would take our case for free. We filed a lawsuit against our insurance company and remained in litigation for three years. This stuff takes forever. Right after I decided to get sober and start my e-commerce business, we got the news that they wanted to settle out of court. The amount ended up being the exact amount we needed for a down payment on a new home. We found a home we loved a month after the settlement was finalized and moved in before Christmas. Things come full circle when you trust the process. We would never have gotten this home we live in right now that we love so much if we had not gone through what we did. I am so grateful, and honestly, I knew we would come out on top all along. My heart was right during the whole process, and I remained thankful during all of it.

That is an example of a time I let go of anxiety and decided to react with peace. What a difference it makes when you let go of fear. I wish I did this easily with everything else, but as a mother and business owner, the tasks never seem to end. When I look at it, my worry is not all that scary, but I have not yet unlearned how to let go of those worries and find a place of peace within it.

After all this, I still ask, Why do we lose so much peace? The only answer I can come up with is because I don't trust God to take care of me. Whenever I try to do things out of my own power, it's like treading water. It never comes full circle like it does when I trust God. I need to accept the fundamental understanding that I cannot control everything around me all the time, that mistakes will happen, and when they happen, I am prepared to forge through them and not let them break me. We are so worried about potential mistakes or potential losses. But if we can understand that a loss is not a loss but rather a lesson learned, then we will approach conflict and work with a much different heart. Once we let go of the expectation that we are in control of the world around us, we can finally enjoy our lives. We need to get comfortable with the worst-case scenario. We need to realize it could happen, and that's okay. For the most part, that is— some dangerous and worst-case scenarios are reasonably feared. But for the regular life stuff, even like losing your home and moving in with your mother-in-law, it's really not as scary as we make it seem.

We live in fast times. Sometimes I daydream of a simple life. You know, about a million years ago when we didn't have phones, taxes, Wi-Fi, bills, kids that asked for all the toys they see YouTubers review. Those must have been peaceful times, at least within themselves. We live in a time in which it is not easy to find peace. We live in a society that caters to stress and anxiety, as if they're glorified. Go to school, go to college, then work for the rest of the days of your life to pay for your college education that gives you a mediocre job that you don't even enjoy. Get married, then stress when things get boring because the media only romanticizes fleeting relationships that go wrong instead of what could go right. We live within a funnel of stress. We are popped into it as babies and slowly swirl around the tornado of "oh shit" until we are old and only have like five minutes to finally enjoy peace.

This is so normal and inescapable. It is something we have to consciously unlearn because we live in a world that normalizes stress as a regular way of life. So yes, I struggle with finding peace and probably always will. I think being aware will help me unlearn my fearfulness in a lot of aspects of life, but with the media, I find it hard to completely ignore it all. Especially when world events are less than comforting.

Lack of peace is just an overproduction of fear. It's self-focused, and it needs to be dealt with and thought about. I feel anxiety in my stomach, so I know when something is wrong. My body always physically reacts to it, which has helped me know when something needs to be dealt with. Sometimes I'm anxious, and I don't even know why, but my body is telling me something is wrong. I'm able to sit and think and run through my worst-case scenario and ask God for help. Figure out how anxiety, worry, and fear manifests in you so that you can see it before it's overwhelming and deal with it.

Some things won't change. Like being a mother. Being a parent is so hard and so stressful. So I have to learn to live with the stress it brings and find out ways to organize my life in a way that makes it flow better. For me, it's mostly my procrastination. If I didn't procrastinate so often, most of my stress would be gone. Still, though, where is this place of peace?

To obtain a moment of peace, we have to be brutally self-aware of what is stealing it. We have to know what drains us and what nourishes us. Ask yourself these questions. Be in tune with yourself to know when you are starting to feel drained, and make time for things that help you unplug: meditation, prayer, singing, cooking, baths, or maybe a walk in the park alone. Now, these things won't flat-out fix your problems, but you need to know what helps you recharge and allows your brain a break. For me, it's baths or showers. The warmth and the sound of running water helps me escape. I'm not sure if I even have any thoughts when I'm showering. I totally zone out and just enjoy the comfort. Find that thing that gives you that boost, and do it once a day if you can.

Recharging and also working on your peace with self-awareness of your fears and anxieties will really start to morph you. There are certain things I will not allow in my brain anymore in the name of peace. One is the worry of people around me being hurt. It's every mother and wife's worst fear to lose a family member. I acknowledge that, but I don't allow myself to entertain or dwell on it. Another one is stressing over money. I don't let that control me anymore. I don't allow the fear of scarcity to dwell in me. When you are no longer controlled by money or the fear of losing things, you can really be thankful for what you have. Be present. Enjoy the present. Don't dwell on the potential future that something you value could be taken away.

CHAPTER 24

EVER A WORK IN PROGRESS

Always be a work in progress.

You cannot be defined by your problems. You need to be defined by how you overcome them. You are not a product of your problems or your hurt. But you are a product of how you deal with them.

Let's say you are homeless, you have mental illness, and you literally have no help from anyone. Even in this situation where the odds are stacked against you, if you succumb to your problems and you admit and believe that "this is my circumstance, and I can't control it," then that's exactly what will happen. You will be a product of your circumstances because you chose it. But if you say, "This is my circumstance, and I'm going to take control of it," then that's exactly what will happen. The power is yours.

And guess what? The "controlling your circumstances" part is not always a physical change at first. Sometimes it's just in our hearts. We cannot physically begin to truly change our life until our hearts are already believing in the change. The actionable result of having money and having a comfortable lifestyle comes *after* we decide to work on ourselves. We don't get the money and lifestyle first, we work on ourselves first, and the rest starts flowing in.

It's basically the law of attraction. If you think your life is shit, then it will keep being shit. But if you think your life is a blessing and you wake up thankful every day and at peace in your heart, then your life will exude that feeling.

I am trying desperately to get you to realize that your heart and mind control your life. That all of this starts in the quietness of your heads. It starts when you decide to not act in anger even though your mother, once again, cut you down with her words. It starts when you decide to love that friend who doesn't have your best interest in mind even though you've been loyal. It starts when you realize that you need to apologize for how you wronged someone. It starts when you realize you maybe haven't been a very nice person at all. It's hard, but we can't gain all we were meant for until we deal with this stuff.

CONCLUSION

HUMILITY TODAY

If you reached the end of this book and felt these messages you already knew or were not helpful, I want you to re-evaluate your pride. For some people, this may be the first time they were met face to face with their pride, and it might have stung a little. It doesn't feel good to know we could be wrong. We may even feel above it, like it does not apply to us In any way.

What I would really love for anyone who is reading this to do, is to decide that there is pride to be uncovered in their heart, and to decide that practicing humility is essential.

If you feel like there was no valuable lesson to take from here, decide there is. Because…well, there is. This is a lesson for the ages and don't let ego tell you any different. Maybe you don't care for my story or even me as a person. Within the web of stories, there is an infinite and eternal truth. That we need to practice humility in order to be properly fulfilled. The message will never and has never changed. Deciding the eternal message of adopting humility into daily practice is something that needs to be done. That being aware constantly of our pride is key to overcoming it.

Now, let's say you *did* come this far and are wondering what next? Does Jessica have any immediate advice on how to practice humility? Ah yes, I do. For starters, watch your thoughts. Catch those negative thoughts and replace them with positive thoughts. Negative thoughts are often inspired by our dwelling on what we lack, don't like, or don't want. If we are focusing on those negative feelings, we are really being ungrateful, and we can't practice humility if we are in an ungrateful place. Now, if something terrible happened, then, once again, *yes, it's okay to mourn*. But still, we can be in mourning and still have things to be grateful for.

Your thoughts are where this all develops. I can't stress enough that your happiness truly lies within your mind. That's it. So actively try to be aware of your thoughts, and pivot them if they stir your heart in a negative way. Pivot them if you know they are wrong. Then, rewrite them to reflect the new truth you want to attain.

Let's say your mom was passive-aggressive toward you . . . again! You keep randomly thinking about it and letting your heart stir over the words she said to you. They were wrong, they were hurtful, and she meant for them to hurt. Stop and breathe. Your mother is imperfect, but she need not control your peace and happiness. You cannot have expectations that your mother will make life easier. Humans cannot create happiness for you. You are the only one stealing your own happiness.

Go blank if you need to get these thoughts out of your head. Turn on a god-awful country song that will help your mind fizzle out of this rabbit hole. Do whatever it is you need to do to get out of this state of negativity. Do something that feels good. Just toss the thoughts out. They have no business in your head. Those thoughts of scarcity belie your truth. There is so much waiting for you, and you just need to decide that scarcity doesn't belong with you anymore and if it pops its head in your head, then you are turning on Beyoncé and saying peace out.

Another word of advice I have is to do something that feels good. If you feel down, go for a walk, dance, sing, shout, cook, clean, sit out in the sunshine, whatever! Just don't sulk. If you feel like you are sulking, taking the first step toward what feels good might be hard, it might feel like you are treading water, but it needs to be done. Don't be so in your head that you can't see the rainbow that awaits you once you get out and start doing an activity that helps you thrive. Mine is being outside in the warm sun. It's always been so soothing for me to just sit in silence and listen to the wind and the cars go by on our street.

Something that often helps change your state of mind is a small project. I have a small garden and a wind chime I make out of seashells that I collect from my beach visits. Repotting a plant or adding seashells to my chime feels like I have accomplished something. Sometimes our brains just need a little bit more dopamine. It can be from something as simple as cleaning, even if it's just organizing your makeup or making your bookshelf nice and neat. It will raise your spirits. It might suck to get to work, but once you do, your heart will be a little lighter.

After that business seminar in December 2018 where Tony Robbins spoke, I went home and realized I was completely stressed about my laundry room. I was so hell-bent on trying to change my state of mind that I cried throughout cleaning the room. It was so much work. I kept imagining what Tony would say if he were coaching me to finish. Somehow it happened. Which was insane considering I had not cleaned it, like, ever. We have *so* much laundry as a family of five, and we basically have this huge bin of clothes that always need to be washed, but we never get around to it; I avoid it like the plague.

A dirty little secret, which is very dirty indeed, is that I hate cleaning. So much. I have always been messy and bad at keeping up with a home. It actually wasn't until recently that large home projects were possible for me. I told my father once that I didn't have it in me to clean but I had all the energy in the world to work on my business. He told me, "It's because you're better at making money than you are at cleaning." My brain kind of exploded. I thought being a clean person was a rite of passage to becoming a real adult. I lived in shame of not being good at it and bad at keeping up with it. I realized there was no reason to be ashamed; I just wasn't made to be good at it.

Changing your state of mind can work. Me, a person who loathes cleaning, somehow accomplished cleaning the messiest room in the home. I honestly didn't believe I was capable. But I went in, and decided I was capable, and decided a part of my burden would be lifted if I just cleaned the damn room. The room's messiness was robbing my peace. I was in control of my peace, and I needed to clean that room pronto.

What I am really trying to get at is protect your peace of mind and weed out the things that prevent it. If it means turning off notifications to that friend that elicits jealousy from you or cleaning your laundry room, just get it out, because it's not serving you, and you cannot serve others if you are always fighting for your own peace of mind.

This brings us to what happens next. After you put down this book. If you're to feel happier and achieve way more than ever in all areas of life, humility cannot simply be a fad. Stir some patience into your humility-in-progress. I've noticed how other entrepreneurs and parents (especially those who are both!) struggle with patience. We look for the new, cool thing to get the job done. A secret key. Well, humility ain't it, fam. It's a daily practice.

And I don't mean practice to imply working hard at it. Understanding humility means you're already practicing it. Because you're now aware of when pride reveals itself. Lasting improvement is the result of daily action. With humility comes love, joy, peace, and all the things. Humble, loving, joyful, peaceful people live better lives, enjoy more flourishing relationships, and want for nothing when it comes to their business or career. Need I say more?

Well, yes, actually. I want to point out that you don't have to wait as long for these results as you might think. Every moment you silence the ego and practice humility, you're going to feel that kindness, that joy. You see situations for what they are and people for who they are, yourself included. Once you get it, you can't not get it. Still, you'll need a side of patience to endure those moments and those relationships to reach your desired destination—lasting fulfillment.

I'll tell you where to focus your practice right away: opinion-sharing. We humans want everyone else to know what we think about everything. But what good is that really doing? Giving others a piece of your mind when they don't ask for it takes away from the relationship. You're making it about what you want to say, not what the other person needs to hear. So hold back when you feel like dishing out. Yup, it's hard. And worth it. Soon you'll see why. Family, friends, clients, and even your own kids will respond so differently when you simply take the time to hear them out without lectures.

So we're clear on this point, let's clarify what I'm *not* saying here, which is that you should keep your true thoughts to yourself and let people walk all over you. No way, José. If you're worried that being humble means getting doormatted, then your concern has nothing to do with humility. That's a vulnerability problem. As in, being vulnerable to the wrong people. Because humility doesn't mean keeping your mouth shut with someone so they can take advantage of you. Or staying quiet when you see something and should say something. Or keeping the peace at a price to your soul. You can be humble with healthy boundaries. There's a balance here, and it may take some time to get right. It'll be worth it. The practice of humility is always worth it. Because it's when you're most humble that you're most empowered to be real with people, influence them in a way that feels good, and become the most respected, most successful version of yourself. All that and more when you're practicing humility.

Strange, I know. But true.

After all . . . it's a paradox.

And I'm okay with that.

GO BEYOND THE BOOK.

Be humble, learn confidence, get paid. Because anything is possible for the soul with humility. I'll show you how to embrace those new opportunities with my personal productivity course *Get It Done*. Check out www.TheHumilityParadox.com for more info.

ACKNOWLEDGEMENTS

I would first like to acknowledge the people closest to me. God, for giving me this amazing life and opportunities. I am amazingly blessed. My husband, Jeffry, and my three boys, Oakley, Judah, and Noah. All four of them have inspired me in different ways and are crucial to my journey. I love you all.

I would also like to acknowledge my mom and dad, Tina and Mike Mooney. Without them, I would not be the person I am today. I also want to reach out my gratitude to my grandparents: my paternal grandmother, Deborah Harris, my maternal grandfather, Tom Healey, and my late grandmother, Gloria Healey. I have a foundation built from stone because of all these people, and I am so grateful for them.

Friends I would love to thank for iningvest into my life are Heather Krenz for being an incredible, godly example and inspiration and Evie Pekich for modeling in the cover photo—and for being a kind and gentle friend.

I would like to thank all the people who left me kind endorsements for my book: Cydne Morgan, Paola Ohlson, Jade Gibson, Arlene Jacobs, Faith Roberts, and Laila Moayer.

I would like to thank Jonathan Hon for helping me step into e-commerce and for being an invaluable piece to my success. I would also like to thank Joshua Lisec for helping me through the whole book process; I couldn't have done it without you! Thank you also to Kerry Miller for all of her hard work doing PR outreach for my book.

I would like to thank every person who has inspired me along the way. Even the littlest bit. Sometimes even small interactions have changed the course of my whole life. I am so thankful for those interactions throughout my whole life that brought me to where I am now. Lastly, I would like to thank every reader who gave me the time of day. I am so thankful and blessed to have your attention.

ABOUT THE AUTHOR

Jessica Bellinger is a professional wedding photographer, e-commerce entrepreneur, and aspiring humble soul. After losing the battle with pride she didn't even know she fought, Jessica surrendered the need we all have to always be right, to get in the last word, and to have all the answers. Jessica realized the secret to victorious living is not self-care, self-love, or self-promotion but hyper self-awareness of our thoughts, emotions, and behavior—and how to change them at will.

Jessica is the author of *The Humility Paradox: How Humble People Can Be Happier, Achieve More, and Make a Better Living*, which teaches that humility brings us what we want out of life with more ease than ego-driven, whatever-it-takes effort. As a uniquely relevant voice, she teaches women entrepreneurs to rebuild their confidence and boost their income by practicing humility in all areas of business—and life.

Jessica was born and raised on Florida's east coast where she and her husband have three boys and two cats. She has never seen snow. Learn about Jessica, check out her businesses, and see her best memes at www.JessicaBellinger.com

CPSIA information can be obtained
at www.ICGtesting.com
Printed in the USA
BVHW032354051120
592627BV00001B/3

- Thank yous for what has been a special but unique journey into parenthood / arrival
  + challenging
- ~~blah blah blah blah~~ (right from the word go we were surrounded by love and support from friends + family)
- 2 years ago / summer if you'd have told us we were living here with our daughter, Rells + Covid - meant all meant + be.
- Joe for housing a May + Joseph situation for our final months in London
  helping out
- moved here - dark, no ceiling lights, wifi down, no TV reception, slid off toilet seat at about 3am total despair - Chavie + family both sides
- I can say without a doubt no one who had a baby in lockdown anywhere in the world, had a cleaner home than we did.
- Abi + Leanne, you had my back throughout the whole pregnancy, always checking in, making sure I was ok, ~~cleaning~~ pack up the flat / entire kitchen

Abi -
Leanne -

-